STUDY G

Lynne Blesz Vestal

HUMAN DEVELOPMENT

FOURTH EDITION

F. Philip Rice
University of Maine

Prentice Hall, Upper Saddle River, New Jersey 07458

©2001 by PRENTICE-HALL, INC.
PEARSON EDUCATION
Upper Saddle River, New Jersey 07458

All rights reserved

10 9 8 7 6 5 4 3 2 1

ISBN 0-13-018569-8

Printed in the United States of America

Table of Contents

Preface to the Student iv

PART ONE — *The Study of Human Development over the Life Span*

1	A Life-Span Developmental Perspective	*1*
2	Theories of Development	*19*

PART TWO — *The Beginnings of Life*

3	Heredity, Environmental Influences, and Prenatal Development	*43*
4	Childbirth and the Neonate	*68*

PART THREE — *Child Development*

5	Perspectives on Child Development	*86*
6	Physical Development	*96*
7	Cognitive Development	*114*
8	Emotional Development	*139*
9	Social Development	*155*

PART FOUR — *Adolescent Development*

10	Perspectives on Adolescent Development	*183*
11	Physical Development	*196*
12	Cognitive Development	*213*
13	Emotional Development	*227*
14	Social Development	*241*

PART FIVE — *Adult Development*

15	Perspectives on Adult Development	*254*
16	Physical Development	*267*
17	Cognitive Development	*292*
18	Emotional Development	*310*
19	Social Development	*325*
20	Death, Dying, and Bereavement	*345*

Preface to the Student

This study guide was prepared for you as an aid in studying and learning from your textbook. It provides chapter summaries, study questions, opportunities for you to define and use key terms, self-test multiple choice questions that cover the material in each chapter, and critical thinking questions that encourage you to assess your own developmental experiences. Use of this study guide in conjunction with your textbook should result in a thorough understanding of child and adolescent development.

The following steps are an effective means of studying:

1. For each chapter in the textbook, first preview the chapter by glancing at the section headings and sub-headings, and at figures, tables, and illustrations. This will begin to familiarize you with what you will be reading, and prepare you for what's ahead. At this point, it might be helpful to look at the *Chapter Outline & Overview* in the study guide and at the *Learning Objectives/Study Questions*. This will give you an idea of what the major points and areas of discussion are in the chapter, and should help you to focus on the important parts as you read.

2. After previewing the chapter, you should thoroughly read each chapter, keeping in mind the learning objectives and questions. You may want to keep the study guide open to the *Learning Objectives/Study Questions* and fill in the answers as you go along. In this way, you can be sure that you have read and understood each major point.

3. After reading each chapter, it is a good idea to sit back and reflect about what you have just read. You may want to think about the material in relation to your own childhood or upbringing, and think about whether the author's presentation of the material agrees with what you would expect. The section in the study guide labeled *Thinking Critically About Your Development* may assist you in this process.

4. The next step is to review the material using the study guide. You should go over the answers that you have already given for the *Learning Objectives/Study Questions* and test yourself on the material. Once you feel comfortable with these answers, go on to the next section, *Key Terms*. For each set of key terms, provide a definition for each term in your own words. Then check your answers at the end of each chapter. Next, the *Applications* section will give you the opportunity to use the key terms as covered in the textbook. Some of these fill-in-the-blank questions reiterate the definitions while others are more conceptual and/or applied. You can fill in the blanks in the study guide and then check your answers at the end of each chapter. After completing these exercises, you should have a thorough understanding of the key terms and how they are used.

5.	An additional way to test yourself on your knowledge of the material in each chapter is to do the *Multiple Choice Questions*. These questions cover the material from the entire chapter. The questions are factual, conceptual, or applied. Thus, various levels of understanding of the material will be required to successfully complete this section of the study guide. You should check your answers with the answers given at the end of each chapter. If you are unclear about any of the answers, then go back to the text and read about it again.

6.	Finally, you are encouraged to complete the section entitled *Critically Thinking About Your Development* as another means of solidifying your comprehension of the material. While there are no clear right or wrong answers to these questions, inability to answer them may indicate an incomplete understanding of the material from the chapter in the text. Also, these critical thinking questions are designed to encourage you to think about the material in the course beyond the confines of the textbook or classroom.

After following these steps, you should have a thorough understanding of the material presented in each chapter, and perhaps gain some insight into your own development as well as those around you. Enjoy the material!

Chapter 1
A LIFE-SPAN DEVELOPMENTAL PERSPECTIVE

CHAPTER OUTLINE & OVERVIEW

I. Introduction to the study of human development

In this course, we seek to describe, explain, predict, and influence the changes that take place in our lives.

II. Periods of development

    A. Prenatal period: includes the development from conception through birth.

    B. Infancy: the first two years
        1. Extends from childbirth through toddlerhood.
        2. Infancy is a period of tremendous changes.

    C. Childhood
        1. Early childhood: 3 to 5 years *[handwritten: sense of self and gender id]*
        2. Middle childhood: 6 to 11 years

    D. Adolescent development
        1. Early adolescence: 12 to 14 years *[handwritten: the form. of positive id]*
        2. Middle or late adolescence: 15 to 19 years

    E. Adult development
        1. Early adulthood: 20s and 30s
        2. Middle adulthood: 40s and 50s *[handwritten: mid-life crisis]*
        3. Late adulthood: 60 and over

III. A philosophy of life-span development

    A. Some important questions – Because of this complexity and of the importance of the subject, a large number of questions are asked in understanding the process of human development.

    B. Development is multidimensional and interdisciplinary. Development can be divided into four basic dimensions: physical, cognitive, emotional, and social development.

    C. Development continues through the life span.

    D. Both heredity (nature) and environment (nurture) influence development.

    E. Development reflects both continuity and discontinuity.

F. Development is cumulative.

G. Development is both controllable and beyond our control.

H. Development reflects both stability and change.

I. Development is variable.

J. Development is sometimes cyclical and repetitive.

K. Development reflects individual differences.

L. Development reflects gender differences.

M. Development reflects cultural and class differences.

N. Developmental influences are reciprocal.

IV. Research in human development: the scientific method – the scientific method involves four major steps:

A. Formulate the problem or the question.

B. Develop a hypothesis.

C. Test the hypothesis.

D. Draw conclusions.

⎫ Scientific method

V. Data collection methods

A. Naturalistic observation - research conducted in a natural environment by watching and then recording behavior without making any effort to manipulate the situation.

B. Interviews - a face-to-face research method in which information is obtained through oral responses to questions.

C. Questionnaires and checklists - research method whereby the subject writes out answers to written questions.

D. Case studies – research method involving in-depth, longitudinal investigations and records of individuals.

    E.   Standardized testing - measures specific characteristics.
         1.   Tests have a high validity if they measure what they claim to measure.
         2.   Tests have a high reliability if the same scores are obtained when the test is administered on two or more occasions, or by two or more examiners.

VI.   Sampling

    A.   The sample is the group of subjects chosen.

    B.   Random samples are often taken from groups enlisted for study.

    C.   Representative sample of a population includes the same percentages of people from the different cultural, ethnic, socioeconomic, and educational backgrounds as contained in the population.

VII.   Experimental methods

    A.   Procedure - In an experiment, the experimenter manipulates variables to determine how they affect one another. Changes are compared with those in control groups that have not been exposed to the variables.

    B.   Independent and dependent variables - The independent variable is the variable over which the experimenter has direct control, and the dependent variable changes as a result of changes in the independent variable.

    C.   Establishing relationships: correlational studies - Experimenters sometimes look at the relationship, or correlation between variables, meaning the extent to which two factors are associated or related to one another.

VIII.   Research designs

    A.   Age, cohort (a group of people born during the same time period), and the time of testing can all affect research findings.

    B.   Cross-sectional studies - Different age groups or cohorts are compared at one time of testing.

    C.   Longitudinal studies - One group of people is studied repeatedly over a period of time.

D. Sequential studies - A combination of cross-sectional and longitudinal research design that attempts to sort out age, cohort, and time effects; age changes are not measured.

E. Cross-cultural research - We have learned about diverse cultures through cross-cultural research. It is important to include information from cross-cultural research when considering theories of development.

F. Ethical issues in research - *Informed consent* and *protection from harm* are two fundamental principles of ethical standards in developmental research.

LEARNING OBJECTIVES/STUDY QUESTIONS

After reading this chapter, you should be able to:

1. Explain what researchers of human development seek to do.

2. Identify and describe the three major developmental periods and their subdivisions.

   a.

   b.

   c.

3. Identify thirteen elements of the philosophy of life-span development.

   a.

   b.

   c.

   d.

   e.

f.

g.

h.

i.

j.

k.

l.

m.

4. Identify the four major steps involved in the scientific method.

a.

b.

c.

d.

5. Identify and describe five types of data collection methods.

a.

b.

c.

d.

e.

6. Distinguish between a random sample and a representative sample.

7. Explain the experimental method.

8. Distinguish between independent and dependent variables.

9. Describe correlational studies.

10. Describe three basic research designs and the advantages and disadvantages of each.

    a.

    b.

    c.

11. Discuss the benefits of conducting cross-cultural research.

12. Discuss some of the ethical issues involved in developmental research.

KEY TERMS I

In your own words, provide a definition for each of the following terms:

1. Prenatal period _____
   _____

2. Infancy _____
   _____

3. Early childhood _____
   _____

4. Middle childhood _____
   _____

5. Adolescence _____
   _____

6. Early adulthood _____
   _____

7. Middle adulthood _____
   _____

8. Late adulthood _____
   _____

9. Physical development _____
_____

10. Cognitive development _____
_____

11. Emotional development _____
_____

12. Social development _____
_____

13. Nature _____
_____

14. Nurture _____
_____

15. Scientific method _____
_____

16. Naturalistic observation _____
_____

17. Interviews _____
_____

18. Questionnaires _____
_____

19. Case studies _____
_____

APPLICATIONS I

For each of the following, fill in the blank with one of the terms listed above.

1. The formation of a positive identity is an important psychosocial task of _adolescence_.

2. A researcher compares IQ scores of identical twins to understand the influence of heredity, or _nature_, and environment, or _nurture_.

3. The _scientific method_ involves a series of steps to obtain accurate data; these include formulating the problem, developing a hypothesis, testing the hypothesis, and drawing conclusions.

4. A researcher unobtrusively observes elementary grade school students during recess and records the number of acts of aggression. The researcher is gathering data by use of _naturalistic observation_.

5. A research method involving in-depth, longitudinal investigations and records of individuals is called the _case study_.

6. A test that measures what it is intended to measure is said to have high _validity_.

7. A test has high _reliability_ if the same scores are obtained when the test is administered on two or more occasions.

8. The _prenatal_ period includes the developmental process from conception through birth.

9. A person experiencing a mid-life crisis is most likely in _middle adulthood_.

10. A child who is beginning to develop a sense of self and a gender identity is most likely in the age period of _early childhood_.

11. The elementary school years correspond with the period of _middle childhood_.

12. The first two years of life is the age period referred to as _infancy_.

13. _Emotional_ development refers to the development of achievement, trust, security, love, and affection.

14. The _social_ dimension of human development includes marriage, parenthood, work, and vocational roles.

15. The dimension of human development which includes genetic foundations for development is called _physical_ development.

KEY TERMS II

In your own words, provide a definition of the following terms:

1. Tests _____
   _____

2. Validity _____
   _____

3. Reliability _____
   _____

4. Sample _____
   _____

5. Random sample _____
   _____

6. Representative sample _____
   _____

7. Experimental methods _____
   _____

8. Independent variable _____
   _____

9. Dependent variable _____
   _____

10. Correlation _____
    _____

11. Cohort _____
    _____

12. Cross-sectional study_____

13. Longitudinal research_____

14. Sequential study_____

APPLICATIONS II

For each of the following, fill in the blank with one of the terms listed above.

1. In an experiment, the variables that the researcher manipulates are called the _independent_ variables.

2. The extent to which two factors are associated or related to one another is called _correlation_, which is indicated statistically from –1.0 to +1.0.

3. Children born during the Depression are said to be of the same _cohort_.

4. A researcher used a sample of people in her study that included the same percentages of the general population of people from different backgrounds. This sample is a _representative_ sample.

5. A test that was designed to measure shyness turned out to be a better measure of verbal ability. This measure would be said to have low _validity_ in terms of shyness.

6. A study in which a group of 3-year-olds and a group of 5-year-olds were compared at the same time for their ability to solve complex problems is a _cross-sectional_ study.

7. A researcher showed one group of children a television program with a lot of violence in it, and another group saw a pleasant show about cats and dogs. The researcher then measured the frequency of aggressive acts that were committed by the two groups. The measure of aggression is the _dependent_ variable.

8. A _longitudinal_ study confounds age and time of testing.

9. A group of adolescents took an intelligence test in March. When they took the test again one month later, their scores were very similar to the first time they took it. This test could be said to have high _reliability_.

11

10. A group of subjects chosen for an experiment are called the __Sample__.

11. When an experimenter closely controls procedures and manipulates variables to determine how one affects the other, the __experimental__ method of gathering scientific data has been used.

12. A combination of cross-sectional and longitudinal research designs that attempts to sort out age, cohort, and time effects is the __sequential__ study.

13. A __random__ sample is often taken from groups enlisted for study.

14. Research instruments used to measure specific characteristics such as intelligence and aptitude are called __tests__.

SELF-TEST MULTIPLE CHOICE QUESTIONS

Circle the best answer for each question.

1. A developmentalist who studies how gross and fine motor skills improve with age specializes in
    a. social development.
    b. physical development.
    c. emotional development.
    d. cognitive development.

2. A developmentalist who studies how memory strategies improve with age specializes in
    a. physical development.
    b. social development.
    c. cognitive development.
    d. emotional development.

3. A researcher conducts extensive, in-depth interviews with a small group of highly gifted children with genius IQ levels, and is interested in applying what he learns from them to how children learn from their environment. What type of study is he conducting?
    a. case study
    b. correlational study
    c. experiment
    d. naturalistic observation

4. A research investigation on cooperative behavior in preschoolers which is conducted in preschool classrooms is an example of a(n)
    a. case study.
    b. naturalistic observation.
    c. interview.
    d. experiment.

5. Bob and Tim are 16-year-old twins. Every year since they were born, an investigator contacts them and they complete a battery of psychological tests. They are participating in a(n)
    a. cross-sectional study.
    b. age cohort study.
    c. sequential study.
    d. **longitudinal study.** *(circled)*

6. What is the first step of the scientific method?
    a. Develop a hypothesis.
    b. Draw conclusions.
    c. **Formulate the problem.** *(circled)*
    d. Test the hypothesis.

7. In an experiment, the conditions that the researcher manipulates are called the
    a. dependent variables.
    b. **independent variables.** *(circled)*
    c. controlled variables.
    d. uncontrolled variables.

8. If a test that is supposed to measure comprehension of algebra does in fact measure algebraic test knowledge, that test is said to be
    a. **valid.** *(circled)*
    b. consistent.
    c. reliable.
    d. repeatable.

9. If the results of an achievement test are influenced by a student's level of stress, the test is considered to have little
    a. validity.
    b. **reliability.** *(circled)*
    c. sensitivity.
    d. predictability.

10. Children who view more cooperative television shows tend to be higher in cooperation, while children who view very few cooperative television shows tend to be very low in cooperation. What correlation exists between watching many hours of cooperative programming and acting cooperatively?
    a. **positive correlation** *(circled)*
    b. negative correlation
    c. zero correlation
    d. unknown correlation

11. A researcher investigates the effect of background music on retaining information. She gives two groups of students material to study. One group studies with background music and the other group studies without background music. She then compares the tests of the two groups. What is the *dependent variable* in the study?
    a. studying
    b. the test scores
    c. the material
    d. background music

12. Which of the following is an example of a cohort?
    a. a group of children of different ages playing together at a playground
    b. a group of children of different ages who were all tested at the same time
    c. a group of siblings who were all tested at the same time
    d. a group of children who were all born in 1987

13. Melissa has a quick temper and she often fights with her sisters. Her sisters have come to expect that Melissa will react negatively, and so they often don't include her in their activities. This makes Melissa even more angry and she fights with them even more. This example demonstrates that
    a. development is continuous.
    b. development is variable.
    c. developmental influences are reciprocal.
    d. development is multidimensional.

14. What is the main advantage of a longitudinal study?
    a. It eliminates cohort effects.
    b. Data for different age groups can be obtained over the same time period.
    c. It is easy to conclude the study quickly.
    d. Subjects are more readily available due to the perceived commitment to the study.

15. A researcher who studies whether aggressive children become violent adults is interested in
    a. the role of genetics versus the role of the environment.
    b. whether development is multidimensional.
    c. the stability of certain personality characteristics over development.
    d. the influence of early traumatic events on later development.

16. A researcher who unobtrusively watches fathers interact with their children on a playground while recording the types of encouragement the fathers give to their children is using what data collection method?
    a. longitudinal
    b. cross-sectional
    c. naturalistic observation
    d. case study

17. Which of the following is *not* a disadvantage of using interviews as a data collection method?
    a. Interviews are very time consuming.
    b. Personal information about individuals cannot be obtained through interviews. ✓
    c. Interviewers need extensive training in order to be non-biased.
    d. Some people tend to be less verbal than others.

18. Cohort effects are those due to
    a. the person's age.
    b. the person's gender.
    c. individual parental upbringing.
    d. the year in which a person is born. ✓

19. A clinician who is interested in obtaining as much information as possible about a patient with unusual symptoms would be best off using which method of data collection?
    a. questionnaire
    b. interview
    c. case study ✓
    d. standardized testing

20. A researcher designed a test for measuring levels of depression, and she wanted to find out if indeed the test really measured individuals' experiences of depression. This researcher is interested in the _____ of the measure.
    a. reliability
    b. validity ✓
    c. sampling
    d. representativeness

21. If a sample is not representative of the population, a researcher cannot
    a. draw conclusions from her data about the general population. ✓
    b. draw conclusions about the group that has been studied.
    c. apply her findings to other groups that are similar to those that have been studied.
    d. use this data to predict later developmental trends.

22. Cause and effect is most easily established in
    a. case studies.
    b. correlational studies.
    c. experimental methods. ✓
    d. nonexperimental methods.

23. A researcher is interested in the effects of age on reading skills. In this example, age would be considered the
    a. dependent variable.
    b. independent variable. ✓
    c. correlational variable.
    d. random variable.

24. A researcher finds a statistical correlation of -.86 between how much television children watch and children's willingness to share. This means that
    a. the more television that children watch, the less likely they are to share.
    b. the more television that children watch, the more likely they are to share.
    c. how much television children watch is not related to their sharing behavior.
    d. watching a lot of television causes children to be less willing to share.

25. A researcher interested in studying how verbal abilities change with age compares first-, third-, fifth-, seventh-, ninth-, and eleventh-graders all in one day. What type of research design did the researcher use?
    a. longitudinal
    b. cohort
    c. cross-sectional
    d. sequential

THINKING CRITICALLY ABOUT YOUR DEVELOPMENT

Integrate material from the chapter with your own developmental experiences to respond to the following items.

1. Identify examples from your own development that support the idea that development reflects both cultural and class differences.

2. Pick a particular age division (e.g., early adolescence) and describe your own development in each of the four dimensions of development: physical, cognitive, emotional, and social.

3. Propose a hypothesis you would like to test about your own development. Develop one of the three basic research designs to test your hypothesis: cross-sectional, longitudinal, or sequential study. What are the advantages/disadvantages of your design?

4. To what cohort do you belong? What economic and social conditions do you share with your cohort?

5. Suppose you are conducting an experiment on how friendships change over the life span. What ethical principles should guide your research design?

ANSWER KEY

APPLICATIONS I

1. adolescence
2. nature, nurture
3. scientific method
4. naturalistic observation
5. case study
6. validity
7. reliability
8. prenatal
9. middle adulthood
10. early childhood
11. middle childhood
12. infancy
13. Emotional
14. social
15. physical

APPLICATIONS II

1. independent variables
2. correlation
3. cohort
4. representative
5. validity
6. cross-sectional
7. dependent
8. longitudinal
9. reliability
10. sample
11. experimental
12. sequential
13. random
14. tests

MULTIPLE CHOICE

1.	b	6.	c	11.	b	16.	c	21.	a
2.	c	7.	b	12.	d	17.	b	22.	c
3.	a	8.	a	13.	c	18.	d	23.	b
4.	b	9.	b	14.	a	19.	c	24.	a
5.	d	10.	a	15.	c	20.	b	25.	c

Chapter 2
THEORIES OF DEVELOPMENT

CHAPTER OUTLINE & OVERVIEW

I. The role of theories

A theory organizes the data, ideas, and hypotheses and states them in coherent, interrelated, general propositions, principles, or laws, which are useful in explaining and predicting phenomena.

II. Psychoanalytic theories

    A. Freud: psychoanalytical theory
1. Sigmund Freud developed psychoanalytical theory which emphasizes the importance of early childhood experiences and unconscious motivations in influencing behavior.
2. Freud used the techniques of free association and dream interpretation to explore inner conflicts between instinctual urges and societal expectations.
3. Personality is composed of three components:
   a. Id - present from birth and consists of the basic instincts and urges that seek immediate gratification, regardless of the consequences.
   b. Ego - begins to develop during the first year of life; consists of mental processes that seek to help the id find expression without getting into trouble.
   c. Superego - develops as a result of parental and societal teaching; it represents those social values that are incorporated into the personality structure of the child. It becomes the conscience that seeks to influence behavior to conform to social expectations.
4. People can relieve anxiety and conflict by using defense mechanisms, which are mental devices that distort reality to minimize psychic pain. The defense mechanisms include:
   a. Repression
   b. Regression
   c. Sublimation
   d. Displacement
   e. Reaction formation
   f. Denial
   g. Rationalization

5. Freud outlined a psychosexual theory of development in which the center of sensual sensitivity shifts from one body zone to another in stages as children mature.
   a. Oral stage (first year of life) - source of pleasure is through sucking, chewing, and biting.
   b. Anal stage (ages 2 to 3) - source of pleasure is through anal activity.
   c. Phallic stage (ages 4 to 5) - source of pleasure shifts to the genitals.
   d. Latency stage (age 6 to puberty) - source of pleasure shifts from self to other persons as the child becomes interested in cultivating the friendship of others.
   e. Genital stage (beginning with sexual maturation and continues through adulthood) - seeks sexual stimulation and satisfaction from a member of the opposite sex.

B. Erikson: psychosocial theory
   1. Erikson disagreed with Freud on several points:
      a. Freud placed too much emphasis on the sexual basis for behavior.
      b. Freud did not place enough emphasis on adult development.
      c. Freud's view of human nature was too cynical.
   2. Erikson divided human development into eight stages and said that the individual has a psychosocial task to master during each stage:
      a. Trust versus distrust (0 to 1 year)
      b. Autonomy versus shame and doubt (1 to 2 years)
      c. Initiative versus guilt (3 to 5 years)
      d. Industry versus inferiority (6 to 11 years)
      e. Identity versus role confusion (12 to 19 years)
      f. Intimacy versus isolation (young adulthood: 20s and 30s)
      g. Generativity versus stagnation (middle adulthood: 40s and 50s)
      h. Integrity versus despair (late adulthood: 60 and over)

C. Evaluation of psychoanalytical theories
   1. Freud's theory helped psychotherapists gain insight into problems and helped to emphasize the importance of early experience, but he overemphasized sexual motivations and had a very cynical view of human nature.
   2. Erikson's theory encompasses the entire life span, but he had an antifemale bias and failed to take into account different social and cultural influences in people's lives.

III. Learning theories

A. Behaviorism
   1. Behaviorism emphasizes the role of environmental influences in shaping behavior.

        2. For the behaviorist, behavior becomes the sum total of learned or conditioned responses to stimuli.
        3. The process of learning is called conditioning.

   B. Pavlov: classical conditioning
        1. Pavlov first discovered the link between stimulus and response in his research on salivation in dogs.
        2. Classical conditioning is a form of learning through association, involving learning to associate stimuli that were not previously associated.
        3. Classical conditioning is a form of learning because our old behavior can be elicited by a new stimulus.

   C. Skinner: operant conditioning
        1. Operant conditioning is a form of learning from the consequences of behavior so that the consequences change the probability of the behavior's occurrence.
        2. Operant conditioning is learning in which the consequences of behavior lead to changes in the probability of that behavior's occurrence.

   D. Bandura: cognitive and social learning theory
        1. Cognitive and social learning theory emphasizes the role of both cognition and environmental influences in development.
        2. Children learn by observing the behavior of others and imitating and modeling their behavior.

   E. Evaluation of learning theories – the emphasis of learning theorists on the role of environmental influences in shaping development has put the responsibility for creating positive environments for child development directly into the hands of parents, teachers, and caregivers; however, they ignore the role of the unconscious and underlying emotions as well as biology and maturation in development.

IV. Humanistic theories - Humanists have a positive view of human nature and believe that humans should be able to reach their full potential as self-actualized persons.

   A. Buhler: developmental phase theory
        1. According to Buhler, the real goal of human beings is the fulfillment they can attain by accomplishment in themselves and in the world.
        2. The basic human tendency is self-actualization.

   B. Maslow: hierarchy of needs theory
        1. Maslow believed that human behavior can be explained as motivation to satisfy needs, such as physiological, safety, love and belongingness, esteem and self-actualization needs.
        2. Maslow also believed that self-actualization is the highest need.

- C. Rogers: personal growth theory
    1. Rogers' client-centered therapy is based on the humanistic principle that if people are given freedom and emotional support to grow, they can develop into fully functioning human beings.
    2. Rogers said that we need unconditional positive regard because we are human beings of worth and dignity.

- D. Evaluation of humanistic theories
    1. Humanists teach people to believe in themselves and assume responsibility for developing their full potential
    2. Humanists have been criticized for being too optimistic.

V. Cognitive theories - Cognition is the act or process of knowing.

- A. Piaget: cognitive development
    1. Piaget used five terms to describe the dynamics of development:
        a. A schema represents a mental structure, the pattern of thinking that a person uses for dealing with a specific situation in the environment.
        b. Assimilation means acquiring new information and incorporating it into current schemas in response to new environmental stimuli.
        c. Accommodation involves adjusting to new information by creating new schemas when the old ones won't do.
        d. Equilibrium is the harmony between sensory information and accumulated knowledge.
        e. Equilibration is defined as a compensation for an external disturbance. Intellectual development becomes a continuous progression moving from one structural disequilibrium to a new, higher, structural equilibrium.
    2. Piaget outlined four stages of cognitive development:
        a. Sensorimotor stage (birth to two years)
        b. Preoperational stage (2 to 7 years)
        c. Concrete operational stage (7 to 11 years)
        d. Formal operation stage (11 years and up)

- B. Information processing - Information processing emphasizes the progressive steps, action, and operations that take place when the person receives, perceives, remembers, thinks about, and uses information.

- C. Evaluation of cognitive theories
    1. Piaget revolutionized developmental psychology by focusing on mental processes and their role in behavior. He has been criticized for underestimating the role of the school and home in fostering cognitive development, and for lack of evidence of discrete developmental stages.
    2. Both Piagetian and information-processing approaches ignore the role of unconscious emotions and emotional conflict as causes of behavior.

IV. Ethological theories

   A. Lorenz: imprinting
      1. Ethology emphasizes that behavior is a product of evolution and is biologically determined.
      2. Lorenz described the process of imprinting, which involves rapidly developing an attachment for the first object seen.

   B. Bonding and attachment theories
      1. There is some evidence to suggest that parent-infant contacts during the early hours and days of life influence later parent-child relationships, although it is not clear that there is a critical period for bonding.
      2. Bowlby suggests that over the first year of life, infants develop attachments to important individuals.

   C. Hinde: sensitive periods of development - Hinde prefers the term sensitive period to the "critical period" in reference to certain times of life when the organism is more affected by particular kinds of experiences.

   D. Evaluation of ethological theories
      1. Ethological theories have emphasized the role of evolution and biology in human development, an emphasis that deserves serious attention.
      2. The ethological emphasis on critical periods of development is too rigid and narrow and the theories overlook the importance of positive environmental influences in overcoming the deficits of early deprivation.

V. An Eclectic Theoretical Orientation – No one theory completely explains human developmental processes or behavior. Rather, each theory contributes something to our understanding of human development.

LEARNING OBJECTIVES/STUDY QUESTIONS

After reading this chapter, you should be able to:

1. Define a theory.

2. Identify important determinants in influencing behavior as proposed by Freudian psychoanalytic theory.

3. Identify and describe Freud's three components of personality:

   a.

   b.

   c.

4. Define the following defense mechanisms:

   a. Repression -

   b. Regression -

   c. Sublimation -

   d. Displacement -

   e. Reaction formation -

   f. Denial -

   g. Rationalization -

5. Outline Freud's psychosexual stages of development:

   a.

   b.

   c.

   d.

   e.

6. Discuss the points on which Freud and Erikson disagreed.

7. Identify and describe Erikson's eight stages of psychosocial development:

   a.

   b.

   c.

   d.

   e.

   f.

   g.

   h.

8. Evaluate psychoanalytical theories.

9. Distinguish between classical and operant conditioning.

   a. Classical conditioning:

   b. Operant conditioning:

10. Describe social learning theory.

11. Evaluate learning theories.

12. Describe the humanistic theories of Buhler, Maslow, and Rogers:

    a. Buhler -

    b. Maslow -

    c. Rogers -

13. Evaluate humanistic theories.

14. Define five Piagetian terms used to describe the dynamics of development:

    a. Schema -

    b. Adaptation -

    c. Assimilation -

    d. Equilibrium -

    e. Equilibration -

15. Identify and describe Piaget's four stages of cognitive development:

    a.

    b.

    c.

    d.

16. Examine the steps involved in information-processing.

17. Evaluate the cognitive theories.

18. Discuss the concepts of ethological theories, including imprinting, bonding, and sensitive periods.

19. Evaluate ethological theories.

20. Define the eclectic theoretical orientation to human development.

KEY TERMS I

In your own words, provide a definition for each of the following terms:

1. Theory_____
_____

2. Psychoanalytical theory_____
_____

3. Free association_____
_____

4. Pleasure principle_____
_____

5. Id_____
_____

6. Ego_____
_____

7. Superego_____
_____

8. Defense mechanisms_____
_____

9. Repression _____
_____

10. Regression _____
_____

11. Sublimation _____
_____

12. Displacement _____
_____

13. Reaction formation _____
_____

14. Denial _____
_____

15. Rationalization _____
_____

16. Psychosexual theory _____
_____

17. Oral stage _____
_____

18. Anal stage _____
_____

19. Phallic stage _____
_____

20. Oedipal complex _____
_____

21. Electra complex _____
_____

22. Latency stage _____
_____

23. Genital stage _____
_____

24. Fixated _____
_____

25. Psychosocial theory _____
_____

26. Trust versus distrust _____
_____

27. Autonomy versus shame and doubt _____
_____

28. Initiative versus guilt _____
_____

29. Industry versus inferiority _____
_____

30. Identity versus role confusion _____
_____

31. Intimacy versus isolation _____
_____

32. Generativity versus stagnation _____
_____

33. Integrity versus despair_____

APPLICATIONS I

For each of the following, fill in the blank with one of the terms listed above.

1. A general model of principles that explains and predicts various aspects of human development, such as Freud's perspective, is called a __theory__.

2. During the psychosexual stage of __phallic__, boys develop an Oedipal complex and girls develop an Electra complex.

3. The psychosexual stage in which the source of sensual gratification centers on the mouth is called the __oral__ stage.

4. After 7-year-old Lauren's baby brother was born, she reverted to thumb sucking to deal with her anxiety about being unloved now that there was another child besides herself. Susan is using the defense mechanism of __regression__.

5. The psychosocial stage in which infants learn that they can trust their caregivers is called __trust versus distrust__.

6. A method in which the patient is encouraged to say anything that comes to mind, allowing unconscious thoughts to slip out, is called __free association__.

7. Freud's personality structure that operates according to the reality principle is called the __ego__.

8. Erikson's psychosocial stage of __initiative vs guilt__ is comparable to Freud's phallic stage.

9. A man who tells his friends that he thinks that cheating on your spouse is immoral, when he himself has been attracted to other women besides his wife, may be using the defense mechanism of __reaction formation__.

10. A student who claims that she failed a test because the teacher doesn't like her, when in fact she hadn't studied, may be engaging in the defense mechanism of __rationalization__.

11. An adolescent who is trying to figure out what she wants to do with her life would be in Erikson's stage of __identity vs. role confusion__.

12. A third-grader who feels badly about himself because he doesn't think that he is as smart as his friends has not successfully resolved Erikson's stage of __industry vs. inferiority__.

13. The Freudian personality structure that operates according to the pleasure principle is called the ___id___.

14. A defense mechanism in which distasteful, unacceptable behavior is replaced with behavior that is socially acceptable is called ___sublimation___.

15. According to Freud, if children receive too much or too little gratification at any given psychosexual stage, they become ___fixated___ at that stage, so that their psychosexual development is incomplete.

KEY TERMS II

In your own words, provide a definition for each of the following terms:

1. Behaviorism

2. Mechanistic or deterministic

3. Conditioning

4. Classical conditioning

5. Operant conditioning

6. Positive reinforcement

7. Social cognitive and learning theory

8. Modeling

9. Vicarious reinforcement_____
_____

10. Humanistic theory_____
_____

11. Holistic view_____
_____

12. Self-actualization_____
_____

13. Client-centered therapy_____
_____

14. Conditional positive regard_____
_____

15. Unconditional positive regard_____
_____

16. Cognition_____
_____

17. Schema_____
_____

18. Adaptation_____
_____

19. Assimilation_____
_____

20. Equilibrium_____
_____

21. Equilibration _____
_____

22. Sensorimotor stage _____
_____

23. Preoperational stage _____
_____

24. Concrete operational stage _____
_____

25. Formal operational stage _____
_____

26. Information-processing approach _____
_____

27. Ethology _____
_____

28. Imprinting _____
_____

29. Bonding _____
_____

30. Attachment theory _____
_____

31. Sensitive period _____
_____

APPLICATIONS II

For each of the following, fill in the blank with one of the terms listed above.

1. The view that behavior is a product of evolution and biology is called **ethology**.

2. After dinner, Jane's father would turn on the dishwasher and then get Jane a bottle. Jane learned to associate the sound of the dishwasher running with getting a bottle, so that whenever the dishwasher was turned on, she began to cry for a bottle. This is an example of **classical** conditioning.

3. The instinct of goslings to follow the first moving object that they see after birth is called **imprinting**.

4. According to Maslow, **self-actualization** is the highest need, and the culmination of life.

5. A person who can use deductive and inductive reasoning has attained Piaget's **formal operational** stage of cognitive development.

6. The **information processing** approach emphasizes the steps, actions, and operations by which persons receive, perceive, remember, think about, and utilize information.

7. It is believed that children must be exposed to language during certain developmental periods in order for them to learn language. These time periods are referred to as **sensitive periods**.

8. Humanists hold a **holistic** view of human development, in which each person is seen as a whole and unique being of independent worth.

9. A child who can use symbols to represent things in the world, but who cannot perform mental operations that are reversible, is in Piaget's **preoperational** stage of cognitive development.

10. The theory of development that emphasizes the role of environmental influences in shaping behavior is known as **behaviorism**.

11. Observing that the positive consequences of another's behavior increases the probability of the behavior in the observer defines **vicarious reinforcement**.

12. Carl Rogers's approach to humanistic therapy, in which the discussion focuses on the client's thoughts and feelings and the therapist creates an atmosphere of acceptance, is called **client-centered therapy**.

13. Elizabeth watched her older brother play soccer. When she was given the opportunity, she kicked the ball and tried to imitate what she had seen during the game. Elizabeth is **modeling** what was seen.

14. A _schema_ represents a mental structure, the pattern of thinking that a person uses for dealing with a specific situation in the environment.

15. Piaget said that children adapt in two ways: _assimilation_ and _accomodation_

SELF-TEST MULTIPLE CHOICE QUESTIONS

Circle the best answer for each question.

1. Chad experienced hunger pains during his science class. Even though he wanted to get up and leave the classroom, he waited until the class was over to get something to eat. Chad is operating on the
    a. oral principle.
    b. reality principle.
    c. pleasure principle.
    d. anal principle.

2. Sam was going to steal candy from a store but feelings of guilt kept him from doing so. His internalization of right and wrong comes from his
    a. id.
    b. ego.
    c. superego.
    d. psychic censor.

3. During what Freudian psychosexual stage does the Oedipus complex and the Electra complex occur?
    a. anal
    b. oral
    c. genital
    d. phallic

4. What is the developmental sequence of Freud's psychosexual stages?
    a. oral, genital, anal, latency, phallic
    b. oral, anal, phallic, latency, genital
    c. genital, phallic, latency, anal, oral
    d. oral, latency, phallic, anal, genital

5. During the phallic stage, pleasure is focused on what body part?
    a. anus
    b. mouth
    c. genitals
    d. hands

36

6. Freud is to _____ as Erikson is to _____.
   a. social; cognitive
   b. cognitive; social
   c. psychosocial; psychosexual
   d. psychosexual; psychosocial

7. Erikson's psychosocial stages of development focus on
   a. pleasurable erogenous zones.
   b. a hierarchy of needs.
   c. conflicts throughout the life span.
   d. infancy and childhood developmental needs.

8. Ann makes sure to meet her infant son's needs for hunger, sleep, and diaper changes, and talks and holds him whenever he needs to be comforted. According to Erikson, her son will learn
   a. trust.
   b. happiness.
   c. autonomy.
   d. identity.

9. Two-year-old Lisa's parents get angry and yell at her for being messy during dinner and while playing with her toys. According to Erikson, Lisa will learn to feel
   a. mistrust.
   b. shame and doubt.
   c. guilt.
   d. inferiority.

10. What is the negative counterpart of generativity?
    a. isolation
    b. stagnation
    c. despair
    d. role confusion

11. Freud is to the oral stage as Erikson is to the stage of
    a. trust versus mistrust.
    b. initiative versus guilt.
    c. intimacy versus isolation.
    d. autonomy versus shame and doubt.

12. In widowhood, Tatiana looked back over her life and was satisfied with how meaningful it had been and was pleased with her involvement with family, friends, and her community. What has Tatiana achieved?
    a. intimacy
    b. identity
    c. integrity
    d. generativity

13. Three-year-old Kayla has been seeing her pediatrician for checkups every six months and fears the shots she receives each time. Now, even though he does not administer the shots, Kayla cries when the pediatrician enters the room because she associates him with receiving shots. Her behavior is a result of
    a. habituation.
    b. social learning.
    c. operant conditioning. Bandura
    d. classical conditioning. Pavlov

14. Eight-year-old Angie is more likely to do her homework if she receives praise from her teacher. This demonstrates
    a. modeling.
    b. shaping.
    c. extinction.
    d. reinforcement.

15. Operant conditioning was introduced by
    a. Freud.
    b. Skinner.
    c. Piaget.
    d. Bandura.

16. According to social learning theory, behavior is learned through
    a. reinforcement.
    b. trial and error.
    c. stimulus substitution.
    d. social interaction with others.

17. What has been described as the "third force" in psychology?
    a. learning theory
    b. cognitive theory
    c. humanistic theory
    d. psychoanalytical theory

18. John observes that his older sister receives praise from their parents for saying "please," so he tries to improve on his manners too. What is this phenomenon called?
    a. classical conditioning
    b. punishment
    c. negative reinforcement
    d. vicarious reinforcement

19. A psychologist who believes that to be a fully functioning individual one should strive to realize his full potential as a self-actualized person is most likely a
    a. humanist.
    b. psychoanalytical theorist.
    c. cognitive theorist.
    d. behaviorist.

20. What is the highest need in Maslow's hierarchy?
    a. esteem
    b. physiological
    c. self-actualization
    d. belongingness

21. According to Rogers, when a person has a poor self-image, she needs
    a. conditional positive regard.
    b. unconditional positive regard.
    c. to learn to accept her real self.
    d. to learn to accept her ideal self.

22. Two-year-old Katherine sees a goat for the first time, and adds another animal to her repertoire of four-legged animals. According to Piaget, this process of interpreting is called
    a. equilibrium.
    b. equilibration.
    c. assimilation.
    d. accommodation.

23. What theorist is associated with cognitive psychology?
    a. Jean Piaget
    b. Carl Rogers
    c. John Watson
    d. Sigmund Freud

24. The emotional tie between the parent and the newborn baby that is created after intimate, physical contact in the first few days of life is referred to as
    a. imprinting.
    b. bonding.
    c. attachment.
    d. sensitivity.

25. A researcher is interested in learning if there is a critical period when a child is biologically most ready to learn verbal skills. She most likely advocates what theoretical perspective?
    a. cognitive theory
    b. ethological theory
    c. information processing theory
    d. psychoanalytical theory

THINKING CRITICALLY ABOUT YOUR DEVELOPMENT

Integrate material from the chapter with your own developmental experiences to respond to the following items.

1. Give an example from your own life of a time when you have used a defense mechanism to relieve anxiety or conflict.

2. Provide an example from your own life of how classical conditioning can work.

3. Learning theorists emphasize the role of environmental influences in shaping development. Provide an example from your own life which tends to support this theory.

4. Maslow arranged human needs into five categories. What need do you direct your energy? What needs have been fulfilled for you? What do you need to do to become self-actualized?

5. Provide an example from your own life in which you have received conditional positive regard as well as unconditional positive regard.

ANSWER KEY

APPLICATIONS I

1. theory
2. phallic
3. oral
4. regression
5. trust versus distrust
6. free association
7. ego
8. initiative versus guilt
9. reaction formation
10. rationalization
11. identity versus role confusion
12. industry versus inferiority
13. id
14. sublimation
15. fixated

APPLICATIONS II

1. ethology
2. classical
3. imprinting
4. self-actualization
5. formal operational
6. information processing
7. sensitive periods
8. holistic
9. preoperational
10. behaviorism
11. vicarious reinforcement
12. client-centered therapy
13. modeling
14. schema
15. assimilation, accommodation

MULTIPLE CHOICE

1. b
2. c
3. d
4. b
5. c
6. d
7. c
8. a
9. b
10. b
11. a
12. c
13. d
14. d
15. b
16. d
17. c
18. d
19. a
20. c
21. b
22. c
23. a
24. b
25. b

Chapter 3
HEREDITY, ENVIRONMENTAL INFLUENCES, AND PRENATAL DEVELOPMENT

CHAPTER OUTLINE & OVERVIEW

I. Reproduction

    A. Spermatogenesis
1. Through repeated cell division (meiosis), about 300 million sperm are produced daily.
2. During intercourse, sperm are ejaculated into the vagina and travel through the uterus and up the fallopian tubes.

    B. Oogenesis - the process by which the female gametes (ova) are ripened in the ovaries.

    C. Conception
1. After the ovum is released (a process called ovulation), it is swept into the fallopian tube. Cilia then propel the ovum toward the uterus.
2. Fertilization of the ovum (or conception) by the sperm takes place in the fallopian tube.

II. Family planning - The goal of family planning is to enable people to have the number of children they want, when they want to have them. Another goal is to prevent the spread of sexually transmitted diseases.

    A. Benefits
1. Protecting the health of the mother and children.
2. Helping the marriage.

    B. Contraceptive use
1. The most commonly reported contraceptive methods are female sterilization and oral contraceptives.
2. The main changes in contraceptive use from 1995 to 1998 were the continued increase in condom use and the sharp decline in the use of the IUD and diaphragm.

III. Prenatal development

    A. Periods of development
1. Germinal period - from conception to implantation (about 14 days).
2. Embryonic period - from 2 weeks to 8 weeks after conception.
3. Fetal period - from 8 weeks through the remainder of the pregnancy.

    B. Germinal period
1. The fertilized ovum is called a zygote.
2. About 30 hours after fertilization, the process of cell division begins.

3. After division, the blastula attaches itself to the inner lining of the uterus in a process called implantation.

C. Embryonic period
1. The embryo is the growing baby from the end of the second week to the end of the eighth week after conception.
2. The head develops before the rest of the body. Many body structures and organs begin to develop; the heart forms and starts beating.

D. Fetal period
1. The fetus has developed the first bone structure, including limbs and digits.
2. By the end of the first trimester, most major organs are present, the head and face are well formed, and a heartbeat can be detected.
3. By the end of the fourth or fifth month, the mother can usually feel fetal movement.
4. At the end of the sixth month, the fetus' eyes are sensitive to light and the fetus can hear sounds.
5. During the third trimester, the head and body become more proportionate.
6. By the end of the ninth month, the skin becomes smooth and is covered with a protective waxy substance called vernix caseosa, preparing the fetus for delivery.

IV. Prenatal care

A. Medical and health care - Early prenatal care is critical since the first three months of fetal development are crucial to the optimum health of the child.

B. Minor side effects - Normal pregnancies may include: nausea, heartburn, flatus, hemorrhoids, constipation, shortness of breath, backache, leg cramps, uterine contractions, insomnia, minor vaginal discharge, and varicose veins.

C. Major complications of pregnancy
1. Pernicious vomiting - prolonged and persistent vomiting may dehydrate the woman and rob her of adequate nutrients for proper fetal growth.
2. Toxemia - characterized by high blood pressure, edema, albumin in the urine, headaches, blurring of vision, and eclampsia. If not treated, toxemia can be fatal to mother and embryo or fetus.
3. Threatened abortion - the first symptom of this condition is usually vaginal bleeding.
4. Placenta abrupto and p lacenta praevia
   a. Placenta abrupto refers to the premature separation of the placenta from the uterine wall.
   b. In placenta praevia, the placenta grows partially or entirely over the cervical opening.

5. Ectopic pregnancy - occurs when the fertilized ovum attaches and grows in an area other than within the uterus.
6. Rh incompatibility - involves an expectant mother with Rh negative blood who carries a fetus with Rh positive blood.

V. Infertility

A. Causes
1. About 20 percent of infertility cases involve both partners.
2. About 40 percent of infertility cases involve the man.
3. About 40 percent of infertility cases involve the woman.

B. Impact
1. Fertility problems can cause significant emotional and psychological distress, including a lack of self-esteem, a loss of sense of control of one's life, depression, grief, anger, and guilt.
2. Some couples report greater marital discord, whereas others say that their problems brought them closer together.

C. Alternate means of conception
1. Artificial insemination - the sperm are injected into the vagina or uterus.
    a. Homologous insemination - artificial insemination with the husband's sperm.
    b. Heterologous insemination - artificial insemination with the sperm of a donor.
2. Surrogate mother - another woman is inseminated with sperm of the man.
3. In vitro fertilization - the egg is removed from the mother, fertilized in the laboratory with the partner's sperm, grown for several days until the uterus is hormonally ready, and then implanted in the uterine wall.
4. Gamete intrafallopian transfer (GIFT) - involves inserting a thin plastic tube carrying the sperm and the egg directly into the fallopian tube, where fertilization is expected to occur.
5. Embryo transplant - a female donor is artificially inseminated with the sperm of an infertile woman's partner; the resulting zygote is transferred, about five days later, into the uterus of the mother-to-be.

VI. Heredity

A. Chromosomes, genes, and DNA
1. Chromosomes in the nucleus of each cell carry the hereditary material called genes, which are made up of DNA, and control the characteristics that are inherited.
2. When the sperm and ovum unite, the 23 single chromosomes within the nucleus of each gamete combine in pairs with those in the other gamete to produce 46 chromosomes in the resulting zygote.

- B. The twenty-third pair and sex determination
  1. Each sperm cell and each ovum contains 23 chromosomes.
  2. Autosomes - the 22 pairs of chromosomes that are responsible for most aspects of the individual's development.
  3. Sex chromosomes - the twenty-third pair of chromosomes determines the gender of the offspring.

- C. Multiple births
  1. Monozygotic (identical) twins - result when an ovum fertilized by one sperm divides during development to produce two embryos.
  2. Dizygotic (fraternal) twins - result when two ova are fertilized by two separate sperm.
  3. Triplets, quadruplets, etc., may be all identical, all fraternal, or a combination of both.

- D. Simple inheritance and dominant-recessive inheritance
  1. The law of dominant inheritance says that when an organism inherits competing traits, only one trait will be expressed. The trait that is expressed is dominant over the other, which is recessive.
  2. Genes that govern alternate expressions of a particular characteristic are called alleles.
  3. An observable trait is called a phenotype, while the underlying pattern is called a genotype.

- E. Incomplete dominance - Sometimes one allele is not completely dominant over the other.

- F. Polygenic inheritance
  1. A polygenic system of inheritance produces a wide variety of phenotypes that may differ from those of either parent.
  2. Reaction range is the inherited range of phenotypes for each genotype.
  3. Canalization is the tendency for a trait to persist regardless of environmental influences.

- G. Sex-linked traits - Some defective, recessive genes are carried on only the twenty-third pair of chromosomes, the sex chromosomes, to produce sex-linked disorders.

VII. Hereditary defects

- A. Causes of birth defects
  1. One in 16 infants is born with some sort of serious defect, or congenital deformity: a defect that is present at the time of birth.

2. Birth defects result from three causes:
    a. Hereditary factors
    b. Faulty environments that prevent the child from developing normally
    c. Birth injuries

B. Genetic defects - Defects may be caused by a single, dominant defective gene, by pairs of recessive genes, or by multiple factors.

C. Chromosomal abnormalities - Can be the result of either sex chromosomal abnormalities or autosomal chromosomal abnormalities.

D. Genetic counseling - Couples at risk for chromosomal abnormalities should discover the possibility of passing on the defect to a child yet to be conceived.

E. Amniocentesis - This procedure involves inserting a hollow needle into the abdomen to obtain a sample of amniotic fluid containing fetal cells, which are cultured for genetic and chemical studies.

F. Sonogram - This procedure uses high-frequency sound waves to obtain a visual image of the fetus' body structure, to see whether growth is normal or whether there are any malformations.

G. Fetoscope - A fetoscope is passed through a narrow tube that is inserted through the abdomen into the uterus to observe the fetus and placenta directly.

H. Chorionic villi sampling (CVS) - This test involves inserting a thin catheter through the vagina and cervix into the uterus, from which a small sample of the chorionic villi is removed for analysis.

VIII. Prenatal environment and influences

A. Teratogens - Teratogens are any substances that cross the placental barrier, harms the embryo or fetus, and cause birth defects.

B. Drugs - Medications, narcotics, sedatives, analgesics, alcohol, tranquilizers, antidepressants, nicotine, marijuana, and cocaine can all harm the fetus.

C. Chemicals, heavy metals, and environmental pollutants - Substances such as dioxin, PCB, lead, and gaseous anesthetics can cause birth defects.

D. Radiation - Radiation from atomic bombing or X-rays can cause problems.

E. Heat - Too much heat can also harm a fetus. If a pregnant woman immerses herself in very hot water, the temperature of the fetus may be raised enough to damage its central nervous system.

F. Maternal diseases - Many bacteria and viruses cross the placental barrier, so if a pregnant woman is infected, her baby becomes infected also.

G. Rubella - If the mother is infected with the virus before the 11th week of pregnancy, the baby is almost certain to be deaf and to have heart defects and visual and intellectual deficiencies.

H. Toxoplasmosis - Toxoplasmosis is a parasite found in uncooked meat and in fecal matter of cats and other animals. The pregnant mother should not change the cat's litter if blood tests reveal that she is not immune. The parasite affects the nervous system of the fetus, resulting in retardation, deafness, and blindness.

I. Sexually transmitted diseases: AIDS
   1. The AIDS virus can cross the placental barrier, so that if the mother is a carrier, there is a substantial risk she will give birth to children with the disease.
   2. About one-fourth of pregnant women who have the infection transmit it to the fetus.

J. Other sexually transmitted diseases
   1. Congenital syphilis is contracted by the fetus of the pregnant woman when the spirochete crosses the placental barrier.
   2. Genital herpes, gonorrhea, and chlamydial infections are transmitted to infants when they pass through the birth canal, so doctors recommend a cesarean section if the woman has an infection.

K. Other diseases - Poliomyelitis, diabetes, tuberculosis, and thyroid disease have all been implicated in problems of fetal development.

L Other maternal factors
   1. Maternal age seems to be associated with the well-being of the fetus. Younger teenage mothers are more likely to have miscarriages, premature birth, and stillbirths than are mothers in their twenties. And women over 35 run progressively greater risks during pregnancy.
   2. Nutrition - A lack of vitamins, minerals, and protein in the diet of the expectant mother may affect the embryo adversely.

IX. Heredity-environment interaction

   A. Studying heredity and environment
      1. Twin studies - Identical and fraternal twins are compared.
      2. Adoption studies - Adopted children are compared to their adoptive parents and their biological parents.

B. Influences on personality and temperament - Heredity not only has an important influence on intelligence, but it also exerts a strong influence on personality and temperament.

C. Some disorders influenced by heredity and environment:
1. Alcoholism
2. Schizophrenia
3. Depression
4. Infantile autism

D. Paternal factors in defects - Paternal factors that may impact the development of the child include paternal age; chronic marijuana use; alcoholism; exposure to radiation, lead, arsenic, mercury, some solvents, and various pesticides or gases; and tobacco smoking.

LEARNING OBJECTIVES/STUDY QUESTIONS

After reading this chapter, you should be able to:

1. Describe the process of conception.

2. List the benefits of family planning and the most commonly reported methods of contraception.

3. Describe the major developments that occur in the three periods of prenatal development.

   a. Germinal period -

   b. Embryonic period -

   c. Fetal period -

4. Identify minor side effects and major complications that may occur during pregnancy.

5. Examine the causes of infertility and discuss the impact of infertility on couples.

6. Identify and describe alternate means of conception for infertility cases.

   a.

   b.

   c.

   d.

   e.

7. Explain our hereditary composition.

8. Explain how the gender of the offspring is determined.

9. Explain how multiple births occur.

10. Describe the process of dominant-recessive inheritance.

11. List some of the sex-linked traits and disorders.

12. List some of the disorders caused by:

    a. dominant genes -

    b. recessive genes -

    c. multiple factors -

13. Identify and describe two types of chromosomal abnormalities that can arise. Provide examples of each.

14. Describe prenatal procedures that can be used to detect defects.

15. Describe environmental factors that can affect the health of the developing fetus.

16. Discuss maternal diseases that can cause birth defects.

17. Discuss how maternal age and nutrition can affect a pregnancy.

18. Identify and describe two methods for sorting out the relative influences of heredity and environment on development.

19. Discuss the influences of heredity on personality and temperament.

20. List some disorders that are influenced by both heredity and environment.

21. Cite paternal factors in birth defects.

KEY TERMS I

In your own words, provide a definition for each of the following terms:

1. Gametes _____

2. Zygote _____

3. Spermatogenesis _____

4. Meiosis _____

5. Oogenesis _____

6. Ova _____

7. Ovulation _____

8. Fertilization or conception _____

9. Germinal period _____

10. Embryonic period _____

11. Fetal period _____

12. Morula _____
_____

13. Blastula _____
_____

14. Blastocyst _____
_____

15. Implantation _____
_____

16. Embryo _____
_____

17. Fetus _____
_____

18. Trimester _____
_____

19. Ectopic pregnancy _____
_____

20. Infertile _____
_____

21. Artificial insemination _____
_____

22. Homologous insemination (AIH) _____
_____

23. Heterologous insemination (AID) _____
_____

24. Surrogate mother _____

25. In vitro fertilization _____

26. Cryopreservation _____

27. Gamete intrafallopian transfer (GIFT) _____

28. Embryo transplant _____

APPLICATIONS I

For each of the following, fill in the blank with one of the terms listed above.

1. The union of sperm and egg is called **conception**.

2. The procedure in which sperm cells and an egg cell are inserted directly into the fallopian tube, where fertilization is expected to occur, is called **gamete intrafallopian transfer**.

3. The process of sperm production that takes place in the testes of the male after he reaches puberty is referred to as **spermatogenesis**.

4. The blastula attaches itself to the uterine wall during the **germinal** period of development.

5. The male sperm cell and the female ovum are referred to as the **gametes**.

6. The process by which female gametes are ripened in the ovaries is called **oogenesis**.

7. Vanessa has her husband's sperm injected into her vagina in an attempt to become pregnant. This procedure is called **homologous insemination**.

8. Monica has the sperm from a donor injected into her vagina in an attempt to become pregnant. This procedure is referred to as **heterologous insemination**.

9. When a blastocyst implants itself in the fallopian tube, the mother is said to have a(n) _ectopic pregnancy_

10. A heartbeat can be detected with a stethoscope in the ~~embryonic~~ _fetal_ period of development.

11. Laura and Mike want to have a child, but Laura is infertile. A female donor is artificially inseminated with Mike's sperm, and after five days, the embryo is removed from the donor and transferred into Laura's uterus. This procedure is called _embryo transplant_

12. The fertilized ovum is called a _zygote_.

13. During the _embryonic_ period, the heart forms and starts beating.

14. The inner layer of the blastula that develops into the embryo is called the _blastocyst_.

15. The procedure of _in vitro_ involves removal of the ovum from the mother and fertilizing it with the father's sperm in the laboratory, then implanting the zygote within the uterine wall.

KEY TERMS II

In your own words, provide a definition for each of the following terms:

1. Chromosomes_____

_____

2. Genes_____

_____

3. DNA_____

_____

4. Autosomes_____

_____

5. Sex chromosomes_____

_____

6. Monozygotic twins _____
_____

7. Dizygotic twins _____
_____

8. Siamese twins _____
_____

9. Law of dominant inheritance _____
_____

10. Dominant gene _____
_____

11. Recessive gene _____
_____

12. Alleles _____
_____

13. Homozygous _____
_____

14. Heterozygous _____
_____

15. Phenotype _____
_____

16. Genotype _____
_____

17. Incomplete dominance _____
_____

18. Polygenic system of inheritance _____

_____

19. Reaction range _____

_____

20. Canalization _____

_____

21. Sex-linked disorders _____

_____

22. Congenital deformity _____

_____

23. Amniocentesis _____

_____

24. Sonogram _____

_____

25. Fetoscope _____

_____

26. Chorionic villi sampling _____

_____

27. Teratogen _____

_____

APPLICATIONS II

For each of the following, fill in the blank with one of the terms listed above.

1. During Tammy's pregnancy, a(n) __Sonogram__ was done, produced from sound waves reflecting a picture of the fetus.

2. When one paired allele is not completely dominant over the other, as in the case of sickle-cell anemia, _incomplete dominance_ has occurred.

3. The tendency for inherited characteristics to persist along a certain path regardless of environmental conditions is referred to as _canalization_.

4. Genes that govern alternate expressions of a particular characteristic (such as skin color) are called _alleles_.

5. Twenty-two of the 23 pairs of chromosomes contained in each sperm and ovum are called _autosomes_; the twenty-third pair are the _sex chromosomes_.

6. Andy and Tom are twins, but they are no more genetically alike than siblings. They are _dizygotic_ twins.

7. Ed and Jeff are twins that developed from the same ovum. They are _monozygotic_ twins.

8. A child who is born with a defective condition such as blindness is said to have a _congenital_ deformity.

9. Rodlike structures in the nucleus of each cell are called _chromosomes_.

10. If George inherits the genes for brown eyes from both of his parents, he would be _homozygous_ for that trait.

11. Your eye color is expressed by your _phenotype_.

12. Barbara has inherited the possibility of having an IQ from 100 to 115. This span of possibilities is referred to as the _reaction range_.

13. The procedure in which a hollow needle is inserted into the mother's abdomen to obtain a sample of fluid containing fetal cells is called _amniocentesis_.

14. A _sonogram_ uses high-frequency sound waves to obtain a visual image of the fetus.

15. Harmful substances that cross the placental barrier, harm the embryo or fetus, and cause birth defects are called _teratogens_.

SELF-TEST MULTIPLE CHOICE QUESTIONS

Circle the best answer for each question.

1. Reproduction begins when a sperm cell fuses with an ovum to form a single new cell. What is this first cell called?
   a. zygote
   b. gamete
   c. autosome
   d. chromosome

2. The sex cells from the mother and father that form a new cell at conception are called
   a. alleles.
   b. gametes.
   c. autosomes.
   d. chromosomes.

3. The twenty-two pairs of chromosomes that are responsible for most aspects of the individual's development, excluding those that determine the gender of the offspring, are called
   a. gametes.
   b. alleles.
   c. autosomes.
   d. acrosomes.

4. What is the duration of the germinal period?
   a. 48 to 72 hours
   b. two weeks
   c. six weeks
   d. seven months

5. During what prenatal stage are the major organs and systems formed?
   a. fetal period
   b. germinal period
   c. zygotic period
   d. embryonic period

6. What is the developmental sequence of prenatal development?
   a. germinal, embryonic, fetal
   b. embryonic, fetal, germinal
   c. fetal, germinal, embryonic
   d. germinal, fetal, embryonic

7. A pregnant woman who has high blood pressure, waterlogging of the tissues, albumin in her urine, headaches, blurry vision, and eclampsia most likely has
   a. toxemia.
   b. placenta praevia.
   c. teratogens.
   d. anoxia.

8. What percent of couples suffer from infertility?
   a. 6 percent
   b. 17 percent
   c. 33 percent
   d. 50 percent

9. What chromosomal pair determines the gender of an offspring?
   a. nineteenth
   b. twentieth
   c. twenty-second
   d. twenty-third

10. When a woman becomes pregnant from the fertilization of two separate ova by two separate sperm, these twins are
    a. dizygotic.
    b. monozygotic.
    c. identical.
    d. non-fraternal.

11. Tom and Forrest are dizygotic twins. Therefore, they
    a. share the same genotype.
    b. resulted from the division of a single fertilized ovum.
    c. come from different environments.
    d. are no more genetically alike than siblings.

12. Which of the following combinations represents a male offspring?
    a. XX
    b. YY
    c. XY
    d. XYY

13. Stacey's father has blue eyes and her mother has brown eyes. Stacey has brown eyes. What is Stacey's phenotype?
    a. blue eyes
    b. brown eyes
    c. two "brown eye" genes
    d. one "brown eye" gene and one "blue eye" gene

14. Andy's parents both have blue eyes, and so does Andy. His eye trait is said to be
    a. **homozygous.**
    b. heterozygous.
    c. multifactorial.
    d. cross-modal.

15. What is a polygenic system of inheritance?
    a. the genetic makeup of a given individual
    b. a trait that is expressed in the individual
    c. **a trait caused by an interaction of gene pairs**
    d. one gene of a gene pair that will cause a particular trait to be expressed

16. Jane has an XO chromosome pattern, a short stature, deafness, and lacks internal reproductive organs. What is her condition?
    a. Down syndrome
    b. **Turner's syndrome**
    c. Fragile X syndrome
    d. Klinefelter's syndrome

17. Which of the following is an example of a sex-linked disorder?
    a. **hemophilia**
    b. Down syndrome
    c. phenylketonuria (PKU)
    d. Tay-Sachs disease

18. Huntington's disease is caused by
    a. **a single, dominant defective gene.**
    b. pairs of recessive genes.
    c. multiple factors.
    d. defective sex chromosomes.

19. What severe genetic disorder occurs primarily among Eastern European Jews, resulting in early death in those children afflicted with it?
    a. Down syndrome
    b. **Tay-Sachs disease**
    c. Klinefelter's syndrome
    d. sickle-cell anemia

20. An XXY pattern indicates what genetic disorder?
    a. Down syndrome
    b. Tay-Sachs disease
    c. sickle-cell anemia
    d. **Klinefelter's syndrome**

21. During Jackie's second trimester of pregnancy, a test for chromosomal abnormalities was performed which involved withdrawing and analyzing amniotic fluid. What is this procedure called?
    a. fetoscope
    b. sonogram
    c. amniocentesis
    d. chorionic villi sampling

22. During Emily's pregnancy, she drank at least three cans of beer daily, on a regular basis. As a result, her baby is at risk for
    a. leukemia.
    b. toxemia.
    c. sterility.
    d. fetal alcohol syndrome.

23. Doctors warn pregnant women not to change the cat's litter because they risk getting
    a. rubella.
    b. toxoplasmosis.
    c. syphilis.
    d. placenta praevia.

24. If a pregnant woman contracts rubella, during which week of pregnancy would rubella have the most adverse consequences?
    a. 8th week
    b. 15th week
    c. 25th week
    d. 40th week

25. Twin studies to sort out environmental versus hereditary effects are based on the premise that
    a. dizygotic twins are more similar genetically than monozygotic twins.
    b. dizygotic twins are 100 percent genetically identical, but monozygotic twins are only 50 percent genetically similar.
    c. dizygotic twins are compared to other siblings because they share the same amount of genetic material.
    d. monozygotic twins are genetically identical while dizygotic twins share the same amount of genetic material as do other siblings.

THINKING CRITICALLY ABOUT YOUR DEVELOPMENT

Integrate material from the chapter with your own developmental experiences to respond to the following items.

1. Talk to your mother (or another woman from your parents' age group) about the advice or warnings she was given by her doctor while she was pregnant. Contrast this information with what we know today about environmental influences on prenatal development.

2. What maternal (paternal) factors would be of concern to you if you were an expecting mother (father)?

3. If someone you know becomes pregnant, what are the most important things that you believe the expecting parents should know about prenatal development?

4. Would you undergo genetic counseling before embarking on a pregnancy? Why or why not?

5. Which personality traits of yours, if any, do you feel were inherited? From whom? What makes you think so?

ANSWER KEY

APPLICATIONS I

1. conception
2. gamete intrafallopian transfer
3. spermatogenesis
4. germinal
5. gametes
6. oogenesis
7. homologous insemination
8. heterologous insemination
9. ectopic pregnancy
10. fetal
11. embryo transplant
12. zygote
13. embryonic
14. blastocyst
15. in vitro fertilization

APPLICATIONS II

1. sonogram
2. incomplete dominance
3. canalization
4. alleles
5. autosomes, sex chromosomes
6. dizygotic
7. monozygotic
8. congenital deformity
9. chromosomes
10. homozygous
11. phenotype
12. reaction range
13. amniocentesis
14. sonogram
15. teratogens

MULTIPLE CHOICE

1. a
2. b
3. c
4. b
5. d
6. a
7. a
8. b
9. d
10. a
11. d
12. c
13. b
14. a
15. c
16. b
17. a
18. a
19. b
20. d
21. c
22. d
23. b
24. a
25. d

Chapter 4
CHILDBIRTH AND THE NEONATE

CHAPTER OUTLINE & OVERVIEW

I. Childbirth

    A. Prepared childbirth - refers to the physical, social, intellectual, and emotional preparation for the birth of a baby.

    B. The Lamaze method of natural childbirth
        1. Important elements
            a. Education about birth
            b. Physical conditioning through exercises
            c. Controlled breathing, providing the psychological technique for pain prevention and the ability to release muscular tension by "letting go"
            d. Emotional support during labor and delivery
        2. Critique
            a. Prepared childbirth is not without its critics, especially if a particular advocate emphasizes a drug-free labor and delivery.
            b. Medical opinion is changing gradually in relation to the role of the father.

    C. Birthing rooms and family-centered care
        1. Birthing rooms are informal, pleasant homelike settings within the hospital.
        2. Birthing centers are separated from, but near, a hospital.

II. Labor

    A. Beginning
        1. Real labor is rhythmic in nature and recurs at fixed intervals.
        2. Sometimes the first sign of labor is rupture of the amniotic sac, followed by a gush of watery fluid from the vagina.

    B. Duration – Labor usually lasts no more than 12 to 14 hours in a woman's first pregnancy and tends to be shorter in subsequent pregnancies.

    C. Stages
        1. The first and longest stage is the dilation stage, during which the mouth of the cervix gradually opens.
        2. The second stage involves the passage of the baby through the birth canal.
        3. The third stage, afterbirth, involves passage of the placenta.

D. Use of anesthesia - Either general anesthesia, which can affect the fetus, or local or regional anesthesia.

E. Fetal monitoring
1. Electronic fetal monitoring, with external devices applied to the woman's abdomen, detects and records fetal heart tones and uterine contractions. External devices are generally used for normal pregnancies.
2. Internal leads may also be used, with an electrode attached to the fetal scalp and a catheter through the cervix into the uterus to measure amniotic fluid pressure. Internal methods are used for high-risk or problem pregnancies.

III. Delivery

A. Normal delivery
1. The head is delivered first, the baby's body then rotates so that one shoulder and then the other is delivered and finally the rest of the baby's body is delivered without difficulty.
2. Normally, it is recommended that an episotomy is performed on almost all patients having their first baby, or on those who have had a previous episiotomy.

B. Stress on the infant
1. Contractions may compress the placenta and umbilical cord periodically, causing some oxygen deprivation during those times.
2. The stress of birth produces large amounts of adrenaline and noradrenaline in the baby's blood.

C. Delivery complications - may include vaginal bleeding during the first stage of labor, abnormal fetal heart rate, breathing problems of the baby after birth, a disproportion in size between the fetus and the pelvic opening, or abnormal fetal presentations and positions.

D. Anoxia and brain injury - Two serious delivery complications are anoxia (oxygen deprivation to the brain) and brain injury.

IV. Postpartum

A. Evaluating neonatal health and behavior
1. Apgar score
a. The Apgar is the most common method used to evaluate the health status of a neonate.
b. The Apgar has designated values for various neonatal signs and permits a tentative and rapid diagnosis of major problems.
c. The Apgar score is composed of five signs: heart rate, respiratory effort, muscle tone, reflex response, and color.

2. Brazelton assessment
   a. Evaluates both the neurological condition and the behavior of the neonate.
   b. The scale assesses four areas of infant behavior: motor behaviors; interactive, adaptive behavior; response to stress; and physiological control.

B. Postpartum blues - After delivery, woman may suffer varying degrees of postpartal depression characterized by feeling of sadness, periods of crying, depressed mood, insomnia, irritability, and fatigue.

C. Cultural factors - Postpartum care that the new mother receives is often very different in the United States from that in other countries.

D. Sexual relationships - Sexual intercourse may be resumed as soon as desired provided that it is comfortable. However, contraceptive measures are required since pregnancy is possible.

E. Returning to work - One consideration following childbirth is whether or not a mother returns to work and the timing of such return.

V. Premature and small-for-gestational-age (SGA) infants

A. Classifications - Each newborn may be classified as full-term, premature, or postmature.

B. Premature infants - born before 37 weeks gestation
   1. Problems relate to immaturity of the organs.
   2. The survival rate of premature infants closely correlates with their birth weight.
   3. Low-birth-weight infants are at elevated risk for adverse developmental outcomes, including impaired cognition, but the outcome depends partly on the home environment in which the child is raised and the IQ of the mother.
   4. Preterm infants can sometimes make up deficits in cognitive, language, and social development during the first 3 years of life.

C. Small-for-gestational-age (SGA) infants
   1. Weight is below the 10th percentile for gestation, whether premature, full-term, or postmature.
   2. Perinatal asphyxia and hypoglycemia can be problems for these infants.
   3. Throughout childhood, children who have been of low birth weight have a greater number of chronic conditions, are hospitalized more often, and generally exhibit a pattern of poorer health than do children who are of normal birth weight.

- D. Parental roles and reactions - The birth of a preterm infant is a stressful event, increased by lack of social supports.

- E. Prevention – The risk of low birth weight is reduced when pregnant women receive more complete prenatal care.

VI. The neonate

- A. Physical appearance and characteristics - At birth, the average full-term American baby is about 20 inches long and weighs about 7 pounds.

- B. Physiological functioning - Newborns breathe on their own, have a strong sucking response, and have difficulty maintaining stable body temperature.

- C. The senses and perception
    1. Vision - Vision is the least developed of the senses, but by six months, visual acuity is about normal.
    2. Hearing - At birth, hearing is only slightly less sensitive than that of adults.
    3. Smell - Newborns are responsive to various odors, including odors from their mother's breast.
    4. Taste - Newborns can discriminate among various taste stimuli.
    5. Touch and pain - There is strong evidence of touch and pain sensitivity.

- D. Reflexes - Reflexes are unlearned behavioral responses to particular stimuli in the environment, for example, rooting and sucking.

- E. Motor activity - Newborns don't have much control over voluntary movements.

- F. Brain and nervous system
    1. New nerve cells continue to form until about the second month after birth.
    2. The nerve cells continue to mature.
    3. Some of the neurons are not yet myelinated.
    4. The newborn's brain is immature, with large areas dysfunctional.

- G. Individual differences - Even in the first few weeks of life, infants show different temperaments.

- H. Stress reactions
    1. Infants show physiological reactions to stress.
    2. Infants show differences in stress reactions during labor itself. These reactions reflect differences in temperament.

LEARNING OBJECTIVES/STUDY QUESTIONS

After reading this chapter, you should be able to:

1. Describe the Lamaze method of natural childbirth.

2. Distinguish between birthing rooms and birthing centers.

3. Describe the three stages of labor.

    a.

    b.

    c.

4. Discuss some of the effects of general and local anesthesias.

5. Discuss some of the complications that can arise during delivery.

6. Idenitfy and discuss two ways to evaluate neonatal health and behavior, including what they measure.

   a.

   b.

7. Discuss postpartum issues, including postpartal depression, cultural factors in postpartum care, sexual relationships, and returning to work.

8. Define the following classifications:

   a. Premature infant -

   b. Full-term infant -

   c. Postmature infant -

9. Discuss problems that can arise when an infant is born prematurely.

10. Discuss problems that can arise for small-for-gestational age infants.

11. Discuss the physical characteristics and the physiological functioning of the neonate.

12. Describe what the neonate's abilities as it pertains to the senses.

    a. Vision -

    b. Hearing -

    c. Smell -

    d. Taste -

    e. Touch -

13. Identify and describe reflexes of the neonate.

14. Discuss differences between the brain and neurons of a neonate and those of a mature adult.

15. Discuss how infants show stress reactions.

KEY TERMS I

In your own words, provide a definition for each of the following terms:

1. Prepared childbirth _____

2. Lamaze method _____

3. Labor _____

4. Show _____

5. Amniotic sac _____

6. General anesthesia _____

7. Local or regional anesthesia _____

8. Episiotomy _____

9. Perineum _____

_____

10. Cesarean section _____

_____

11. Anoxia _____

_____

12. Prolapsed umbilical cord _____

_____

APPLICATIONS I

For each of the following, fill in the blank with one of the terms listed above.

1. A woman who discharges blood-tinged mucous shortly before labor begins has experienced the __Show__.

2. A woman who begins to experience uterine contractions at fixed intervals of about 15 minutes apart is in __labor__.

3. Throughout her pregnancy, Sandra and her husband got a nursery ready for the baby's arrival, took Lamaze classes, read about parenting, exercised and ate healthy, and discussed parenting issues they would face. Their preparation for the birth of their baby is called __prepared childbirth__.

4. If a pregnant woman cannot deliver her baby vaginally, the doctor may perform a __C-section__ and remove the baby surgically.

5. If the umbilical cord is squeezed between the baby's body and the birth canal, the baby may experience oxygen deprivation to the brain, or __anoxia__.

6. If a pregnant woman experiences a gush of watery fluid from her vagina, then her __amniotic sac__ has ruptured.

7. The underlying feature of the __Lamaze__ method is its focus on teaching the woman that she can be in control during the experience.

8. Anesthesia that crosses the placental barrier and can decrease the responsiveness of the newborn baby is called a __general__ anesthesia.

9. In order to prevent excessive tearing of the tissues of the __perineum__, doctors usually perform a(n) __episiotomy__ during childbirth.

10. A type of anesthesia that blocks pain in specific areas and has a minimal effect on the baby is called a __local__ anesthesia.

KEY TERMS II

In your own words, provide a definition for each of the following terms:

1. Apgar score

2. Brazelton Neonatal Behavior Assessment Scale

3. Postpartal depression

4. Full-term infant

5. Premature infant

6. Postmature infant

7. Vernix caseosa

8. Colostrum

9. Reflexes

10. Neurons _____

APPLICATIONS II

For each of the following, fill in the blank with one of the terms listed above.

1. A child is given a value called the __Apgar score__ at one minute and again at 5 minutes after birth.

2. A __full-term__ infant is one whose gestational age is 37 to 42 weeks.

3. A __premature__ infant is one whose gestational age is less than 37 weeks old.

4. A few days after bringing her newborn baby home, Sarah felt very sad, and had bouts of crying and irritability. She was probably suffering from __postpartal depression__.

5. The __neurons__ serve to transmit messages from one to another in the nervous system.

6. A newborn's skin is covered with a protective cheeselike substance called __vernix caseosa__.

7. If a doctor wants to know how a newborn's central nervous system is functioning, she could use the __Brazelton__.

8. In the first 2 to 3 days after birth, a high-protein liquid secreted by the mother's breasts prior to her milk coming in, called __colostrum__, contains antibodies to protect the nursing infant from diseases.

9. Bill was born after 42 weeks. He is classified as a _____ infant.

10. Some __reflexes__ have developed through evolution in order to protect the baby from physical discomfort or from falling.

SELF-TEST MULTIPLE CHOICE QUESTIONS

Circle the best answer for each question.

1. What is the longest stage of labor?
   a. first
   b. second
   c. third
   d. fourth

2. Afterbirth refers to the
   a. first stage of labor.
   b. second stage of labor.
   c. third stage of labor.
   d. first month after birth.

3. When Kathy went into labor with twins, the obstetrician attached an electrode to the fetal scalps and a catheter through the cervix into the uterus to measure amniotic fluid pressure. What is this procedure called?
   a. episiotomy
   b. fetal monitoring
   c. amniocentesis
   d. forceps delivery

4. Which of the following is *not* assessed by the Brazelton Neonatal Behavior Assessment Scale?
   a. motor behaviors
   b. intermodal perception
   c. response to stress
   d. interactive, adaptive behavior

5. Steve and Ann Marie attend a series of weekly childbirth training classes focusing on breathing techniques, relaxation exercises, and Steve's full participation in the process. Which childbirth strategy has this couple selected?
   a. Lamaze method
   b. standard method
   c. Leboyer method
   d. cesarean method

6. Birthing facilities that offer the comfort of a homelike atmosphere with the medical backup of a nearby hospital are called
   a. birthing rooms.
   b. labor and delivery rooms.
   c. Lamaze centers.
   d. birthing centers.

7. Discharge of the blood-tinged mucous plug that seals the neck of the uterus is called
   a. labor.
   b. show.
   c. a contraction.
   d. dilation.

8. Research suggests that the reason many babies are born alert is that
   a. there is a change in temperature from the womb to air.
   b. they are startled by the noises when they are first born.
   c. they are affected by the bright lights in the delivery room.
   d. the stress of birth stimulates production of adrenaline and noradrenaline.

9. Which response is *not* recorded on the Brazelton Neonatal Behavioral Assessment Scale?
   a. hand-to-mouth coordination
   b. interactive, adaptive behavior
   c. response to stress
   d. respiratory effort

10. Over a period of several hours, Ann's cervix is gradually opening. Ann is in which stage of labor?
    a. first
    b. second
    c. third
    d. fourth

11. During Maria's second stage of labor, her obstetrician made an incision of the perineum to allow for passage of the baby from the birth canal without tearing the mother's tissue. What is this procedure called?
    a. episiotomy
    b. cesarean section
    c. Lamaze method
    d. forceps delivery

12. During labor, Frances is experiencing her newborn's umbilical cord and placenta being expelled. This occurs during what stage of labor?
    a. first
    b. second
    c. third
    d. fourth

13. Electronic fetal monitoring with internal leads is generally used
    a. for most routine normal pregnancies.
    b. during normal pregnancies when parents want to monitor the pregnancy at all times.
    c. when problems with the pregnancy are anticipated.
    d. when doctors want to restrict the movement of the baby.

14. When is the Apgar score taken?
    a. at 1 minute and again at 5 minutes after the baby's birth
    b. at 1 hour after the baby's birth
    c. at 1 hour and again at 24 hours after the baby's birth
    d. at 24 hours, 48 hours, and 72 hours after the baby's birth

15. A newborn receives a perfect score on the Apgar. What was her score?
    a. 0
    b. 1
    c. 7
    d. 10

16. Kyle was born buttocks first. This is called
    a. breech position.
    b. transverse position.
    c. cesarean section.
    d. anoxia delivery.

17. At birth, the average full-term baby in the United States is about _____ inches long and weighs about _____ pounds.
    a. 22.5; 5.5
    b. 22; 7
    c. 20; 5.5
    d. 20; 7

18. Jodie developed physiological jaundice as a newborn. She was probably treated by
    a. placing her in intensive care and closely monitoring her heart rate and breathing.
    b. maintaining her body temperature at a constant rate.
    c. placing her under fluorescent lights.
    d. bathing her in a warm saline bath.

19. Immediately following birth, the newborn is covered with a waxy substance that is quickly cleaned away. What is this substance called?
    a. lanugo
    b. meconium
    c. vernix caseosa
    d. amniotic fluid

20. Joshua was born prematurely, which means that he
    a. was born before 37 weeks gestation.
    b. weighed less than 2,500 grams.
    c. weighed 90 percent or less than the average weight of infants of the same gestational age.
    d. was born after 42 weeks gestation.

21. What is an unlearned behavior response to a particular stimulus in the environment called?
    a. reflex
    b. habit
    c. reaction
    d. response

22. When Finn's mother dropped a book on the floor, he reacted by extending his arms to the side, with his fingers outstretched as if to catch onto something. What reflex did he use?
    a. grasping reflex
    b. rooting reflex
    c. Moro reflex
    d. Babinski reflex

23. A pediatrician strokes the soles of an infant's feet from heel to toes. The infant spreads and raises his toes upward. What reflex does the pediatrician observe?
    a. Babkin reflex
    b. Moro reflex
    c. Palmar grasp reflex
    d. Babinski reflex

24. The Apgar scale evaluates all of the following qualities, *except*
    a. heart rate.
    b. respiratory effort.
    c. reflex response.
    d. body temperature.

25. A mother gently touches her infant daughter's cheek with finger pressure. What newborn reflex will she elicit?
    a. rooting
    b. sucking
    c. grasping
    d. Babinski

THINKING CRITICALLY ABOUT YOUR DEVELOPMENT

Integrate material from the chapter with your own developmental experiences to respond to the following items.

1. Compare and contrast the relatively new ideas of birthing rooms and birthing centers with the environment in which you were born.

2. Was the Lamaze method of natural childbirth considered as an option when you were born? Why or why not?

3. Based on research findings that demonstrate the occurrence of prenatal learning, to what extent would you try to teach your baby in utero?

4. Based on what you have read in this chapter, what concerns would you have about postpartum issues, such as returning to work, if you were an expecting parent?

5. Report on the maternity leave policy at your place of employment. If you are a full-time student, report on the maternity leave policy for employees of your school.

ANSWER KEY

APPLICATIONS I

1. show
2. labor
3. prepared childbirth
4. cesarean section
5. anoxia
6. amniotic sac
7. Lamaze
8. general
9. perineum, episiotomy
10. local or regional

APPLICATIONS II

1. Apgar score
2. full-term
3. premature
4. postpartal depression
5. neurons
6. vernix caseosa
7. Brazelton Neonatal Behavior Assessment Scale
8. colostrum
9. premature
10. reflexes

MULTIPLE CHOICE

1. a	6. d	11. a	16. a	21. a
2. c	7. b	12. c	17. d	22. c
3. b	8. d	13. c	18. c	23. d
4. b	9. d	14. a	19. c	24. d
5. a	10. a	15. d	20. a	25. a

Chapter 5
PERSPECTIVES ON CHILD DEVELOPMENT

CHAPTER OUTLINE & OVERVIEW

I. Child development as a subject of study

   Child development is a specialized discipline devoted to the understanding of all aspects of human development from birth to adolescence.

II. Historical perspectives

   A. Children as miniature adults - During the Middle Ages and until several hundred years later, childhood was not considered a separate stage of life and children were expected to be little adults.

   B. Children as burdens - Before modern birth control was available, children who were not wanted were often considered to be a burden, and were often placed in orphanages where many of them died.

   C. Utilitarian value of children - Until the twentieth century, children were often abusively used as child laborers; England passed the first child labor laws in 1832.

III. Early philosophies regarding the moral nature of children

   A. Original sin
      1. According to the Christian doctrine of original sin, children were born sinful and rebellious, and were in desperate need of redemption. The parents' role was to break the rebellious spirit through strict discipline.
      2. In contrast, Horace Bushnell emphasized that God's love and grace are mediated through caring parents; this view was the forerunner of modern concepts of child development.

   B. Tabula rasa: John Locke - According to Locke, children are born a "blank slate," neither good nor bad, and how they turn out depends on what they experience while growing up.

   C. Noble savages: Jean-Jacques Rousseau
      1. Children are endowed with a sense of right and wrong.
      2. There are four stages of development: infancy, childhood, late childhood, and adolescence, and parents should be responsive to the child's needs at each stage.
      3. Rousseau emphasized maturation.

IV. Evolutionary biology

　　A.　Origin of species: Charles Darwin
　　　　1.　The human species has evolved over millions of years through the process of natural selection and the survival of the fittest.
　　　　2.　Darwin's four major contributions:
　　　　　　a.　Humans are kin to all living things.
　　　　　　b.　Individual differences are important.
　　　　　　c.　Behavior is adaptive.
　　　　　　d.　The scientific observation in gathering data is important.

V. Baby biographies

　　A.　During the late nineteenth and early twentieth centuries, children were studied by keeping biographical records of their behavior.

　　B.　These records were not objectives, but they were the forerunners of later observations that tried to describe normal growth patterns during various stages of development.

VI. Normative studies

　　A.　The contents of children's minds: G. Stanley Hall - Hall began the movement of normative studies by having children answer questionnaires about their lives.

　　B.　Growth patterns: Arnold Gesell
　　　　1.　Gesell wrote volumes about typical motor development, social behavior, and personality traits.
　　　　2.　Gesell emphasized the role of biological maturation in determining development.

　　C.　Intelligence testing: Lewis Terman - Terman published the first widely used intelligence test in the United States, the Stanford-Binet Intelligence Scale.

VII. Modern contributions to child development

　　A.　Research centers - Interest in research in child development blossomed after World War I, and a number of centers opened across the United States.

　　B.　Medical and mental health practitioners
　　　　1.　Medical and child guidance practitioners have provided much information about child development.
　　　　2.　A new field, called developmental pediatrics, has emerged, which integrates medical and psychological knowledge.

C. Today - Although we have considerable medical and psychological knowledge, we are still lacking in areas such as adequate child care for working parents, and prevention of child abuse and infant mortality.

LEARNING OBJECTIVES/STUDY QUESTIONS

After reading this chapter, you should be able to:

1. Describe the discipline of child development.

2. Describe the following historical perspectives on children's development:

    a. Children are seen as miniature adults.

    b. Children are considered burdens.

    c. There is a utilitarian value of children.

3. Describe the following early philosophies of the moral nature of children:

    a. Original sin -

    b. Tabula rasa -

    c. Noble savages -

4. Describe Darwin's concepts of natural selection and survival of the fittest. What aspects of Darwin's theory are still maintained today?

5. Discuss the contributions to child development by Hall, Gesell, and Terman.

6. Discuss modern contributions to child development. What still needs to be improved?

KEY TERMS

In your own words, provide a definition for each of the following terms:

1. Child development_____

_____

2. Original sin_____

_____

3. Tabula rasa_____

_____

4. Noble savages_____

_____

5. Maturation _____

6. Natural selection _____

7. Survival of the fittest _____

8. Developmental pediatrics _____

APPLICATIONS

For each of the following, fill in the blank with a term listed above.

1. A person who believes that children are born morally neutral and will develop based on their experiences in the world might agree with Locke that children are a *tabula rasa*

2. A new field of study that integrates medical knowledge, psychological understanding, health care, and parental guidance in relation to children is called *developmental pediatrics*

3. A specialized discipline devoted to all aspects of human growth from birth to adolescence is called *child development*

4. Rousseau believed that children know what is right and wrong and thus he considered them to be *noble savages*

5. Darwin's notion that only the fittest live to pass on their superior traits to future generations is referred to as *survival of the fittest*

6. The idea that certain species survived because they had adaptive characteristics is the theory of *natural selection*

7. A person who believes that children are born sinful and need to be saved may subscribe to the doctrine of *original sin*

8. The unfolding of the genetically determined patterns of growth and development is referred to as *maturation*

SELF-TEST MULTIPLE CHOICE QUESTIONS

Circle the best answer for each question.

1. Child development is a specialized discipline devoted to the understanding of all aspects of human growth from
    a. prenatal development to late childhood.
    b. birth to late childhood.
    c. birth to adolescence.
    d. birth to death.

2. The first child labor laws were passed in
    a. 1642.
    b. 1756.
    c. 1789.
    d. 1832.

3. Belief in the doctrine of original sin may have led parents to
    a. nurture their children in a warm and caring fashion.
    b. use harsh punishments for their children.
    c. reject Christian beliefs in God as the savior.
    d. believe that their children were inherently good.

4. Horace Bushnell believed that
    a. all children were born inherently sinful and were in need of redemption.
    b. children should have caring and loving parents who guide them in what is right and wrong.
    c. parents' major role in moral development is praying for their children's salvation.
    d. parents should use strict punishment to break a child of sinfulness.

5. Philosophers who believe that children are born as a tabula rasa believe that children are born
    a. inherently good.
    b. inherently bad.
    c. morally neutral.
    d. with original sin.

6. Who first emphasized the role of maturation in development?
    a. Rousseau
    b. Darwin
    c. Locke
    d. Terman

7. The survival of giraffes and the demise of animals with shorter necks who lived on plains where the major source of food was from the leaves on the tall trees is an example of
   a. recapitulation theory.
   b. maturational theory.
   c. tabula rasa.
   d. the process of natural selection.

8. Who viewed children as noble savages, endowed with a sense of right and wrong?
   a. John Locke
   b. G. Stanley Hall
   c. Charles Darwin
   d. Jean-Jacques Rousseau

9. Who proposed that the human species had evolved over millions of years through the process of natural selection and the survival of the fittest?
   a. Hall
   b. Locke
   c. Darwin
   d. Gesell

10. Which of the following was *not* an early philosophy regarding the moral nature of children?
    a. morality of constraint
    b. tabula rasa
    c. original sin
    d. noble savages

11. Which theorist believed that socialization could not overcome the effects of maturation on development?
    a. G. Stanley Hall
    b. Arnold Gesell
    c. Lewis Terman
    d. Charles Darwin

12. The first intelligence test, designed by Binet in Paris, was intended to
    a. identify retarded children in the school system.
    b. determine which children should enter private schools for gifted children.
    c. identify which children needed special help in social adjustment to new situations.
    d. All of the answers are correct.

13. Who said children were a *tabula rasa*, a "blank slate"?
    a. Locke
    b. Hall
    c. Gesell
    d. Darwin

14. Who was the first to emphasize maturation?
    a. Darwin
    b. Gesell
    c. Locke
    d. Rousseau

15. G. Stanley Hall is noted for his use of _____ in the study of child development.
    a. questionnaires
    b. case studies
    c. adoption studies
    d. identical twins reared apart studies

THINKING CRITICALLY ABOUT YOUR DEVELOPMENT

Integrate material from the chapter with your own developmental experiences to respond to the following items.

1. Even though they were portrayed as "historical perspectives" in the text, describe news stories that you have heard that reveal how some children today are treated as:

    a. Miniature adults -

    b. Burdens -

    c. Laborers -

2. Discuss your reaction to Rousseau's notion that children are "noble savages," endowed with a sense of right and wrong. Is there anything in your experience with children to suggest that Rousseau was either right or wrong?

3. Discuss your reaction to John Locke's idea that children are morally neutral, with no inborn tendencies, or as he put it, a "tabula rasa." Is there anything in your experience with children to suggest that Locke was either right or wrong?

4. Interest in child development has grown considerably over the years. In what fields do we now have child specialists that didn't exist before? What specialists have you benefited from?

5. There is a great need for adequate child care for working parents. What suggestions do you have for adequate child care?

6. What do you see as the most pressing child development issues facing our society today?

ANSWER KEY

APPLICATIONS

1. tabula rasa
2. developmental pediatrics
3. child development
4. noble savages
5. survival of the fittest
6. natural selection
7. original sin
8. maturation

MULTIPLE CHOICE

1. c
2. d
3. b
4. b
5. c
6. a
7. d
8. d
9. c
10. a
11. b
12. a
13. a
14. d
15. a

Chapter 6
PHYSICAL DEVELOPMENT

CHAPTER OUTLINE & OVERVIEW

I. Physical growth

    A. Body height and weight
        1. Growth from birth to adolescence occurs in two different patterns:
            a. The first pattern is one of very rapid but decelerating growth.
            b. The second pattern shows a more linear and steadier annual increment.
        2. During puberty, growth spurts are evident for boys and girls.

    B. Individual differences - There are wide differences in growth patterns, influenced by heredity, nutrition, health care, and cultural and ethnic differences.

    C. Body proportions - Not all parts of the body grow at the same rate.
        1. Cephalocaudal principle - Growth proceeds downward from the head to the feet.
        2. Proximodistal principle - Growth proceeds from the center of the body outward to the extremities.

    D. Organ systems - The lymphoid system, the reproductive system, and the central nervous system do not follow the general pattern of growth.

    E. Brain growth and nerve maturation
        1. Not only does the brain grow in size, but also increasingly complex nerve pathways and connections among nerve cells develop so that the central nervous system is able to perform more complex functions.
        2. There is an increase in myelinization of individual neurons.
        3. The cerebral cortex contains the higher brain centers controlling intellectual, sensory, and motor functions. The two sides of the brain each perform specialized functions.
        4. Different regions of the cortex mature at different rates. The motor area of the cortex matures first, followed by the sensory area, and then the association areas. Broca's area is involved in speech and Wernicke's area is involved in understanding language.

    F. Teeth eruption times - The timing of teeth eruption is somewhat variable, depending on heredity and nutrition.

II. Motor development

    A. Gross-motor skills and locomotion during infancy - Motor development is dependent primarily on overall physical maturation, especially on skeletal and neuromuscular development.

    B. Fine-motor skills during infancy - These are the skills using the smaller muscles of the body, such as reaching and grasping.

    C. Gross-motor skills of preschool children - Preschool children show increased skill and mastery of their bodies in performing physical feats.

    D. Fine-motor skills of preschool children - Preschool children become more adept at performing activities that involve a high degree of small-muscle and eye-hand coordination.

    E. Handedness - Handedness develops slowly and is not always consistent in the early years.

    F. Changes during the school years
        1. There is an increase in motor abilities as their bodies continue to grow, as well as improvement in fine motor skills.
        2. There are inconsistent gender differences in motor development between boys and girls during middle childhood. Prior to puberty, many of these differences in motor skills are due to differential expectations and experiences of boys and girls.
        3. Older children have a decided advantage over younger children in sports that require quick reactions. Adults are better still.

    G. Physical fitness - Today's school children are less physically fit than were children in the 1960s because they are not active enough.

III. Physically handicapped children

    A. Speech-handicapped children - Speech handicaps are among the most common of all physical handicaps in children and may be due to congenital malformations, or arise as a consequence of hearing, neurological, or developmental problems.

    B. Hearing-handicapped children - Hearing problems may not be discovered until the child is 1 or 2 years old.

    C. Visually handicapped children - Blindness may be congenital or may develop gradually or suddenly from a wide variety of causes. Visually handicapped infants usually lag behind sighted infants in mobility and locomotion.

D. Children with skeletal, orthopedic, or motor-skills handicaps - These types of handicaps range from almost complete disability to minor orthopedic or motor skill dysfunctions.

E. Adjustments - Handicapped children may be subject to cruel teasing by other children.

F. Family Coping – Raising children with disabilities places a great deal of stress on the family. All such families have to learn to cope the best way they can.

G. Education - In 1975, federal law in the United States mandated that all children, regardless of their handicap, receive public education in the least restrictive environment that is educationally sound.

IV. Perceptual development

    A. Depth perception
       1. Depth perception develops very early in infancy.
       2. Not only do children develop the perception of depth, but they also develop the ability to portray depth

    B. Perception of form and motion
       1. During the first two years of life, the way that infants perceive the form of objects changes.
       2. Infants have the ability to perceive objects with more than one sense.

    C. Perception of the human face - Infants prefer to look at human faces over objects.

    D. Auditory perception
       1. Auditory perception depends on four factors: auditory acuity, the ability to detect sound of different frequencies, sound localization, and gap detection.
       2. Sound localization improves substantially during the first year after birth, with an especially high rate of change during the first half-year.
       3. The minimum detectable gap, called the gap threshold, is considerably worse for 3- and 6-month-olds than for adults, indicating that gap-detection abilities are quite poor in infants.

V. Nutrition

    A. Breast-feeding versus bottle-feeding - Breast-feeding declined rapidly in popularity over this century, but recently has been gaining in popularity again.
       1. Advantages - Breast milk is the most nutritious food available; it contains antibodies that immunize the infant from disease; it helps shrink the uterus back to normal size more quickly; it is convenient; and there are psychological advantages.

2. Disadvantages - It can limit the mother's freedom; exclude the father from feeding; some drugs and chemicals can be passed to the baby; some mothers do not produce enough milk to satisfy the baby; and for some, breast-feeding is painful.
3. Personal choice - One of the most important considerations is the mother's attitude toward nursing itself.

B. Dietary requirements
1. A balanced diet is necessary for good health and vigor.
2. Dietary nutrients are derived from four basic food groups: milk and dairy products, meat, fruits and vegetables, and breads and cereals.
3. Consuming breakfast generally has a short-term positive effect on basic cognitive processes.

C. Obesity - Obesity can be due to many factors, such as heredity, eating habits, activity level, and psychological factors.

D. Malnutrition - An inadequate diet, such as in the extreme case of marasmus, may lead to mental retardation and other serious problems. Kwashiorkor results when there is a protein deficiency.

E. What is safe to eat? - Children do not always understand what objects are appropriate to eat. Poisoning and choking result.

VI. Sleep

A. Needs
1. If infants are comfortable, they will get the amount of sleep they need; in contrast, 2-year-olds won't. Resistance to going to bed peaks between 1 to 2 years, and may be due to separation anxiety.
2. Parents need to develop regular sleeping habits for their children.

B. Habits – There are several things that parents can do to develop regular sleeping habits for their children:
1. Put children to bed at the same time every night.
2. Develop a relaxed bedtime routine.
3. Avoid excessive stimulation before bedtime.
4. Keep bedtime relaxed and happy.
5. Avoid sending children to bed as a means of discipline.
6. Avoid frightening stories or television programs.

VII. Health care

A. Health supervision of the well child - Supervision by medical personnel should include instruction of parents in child development, routine immunizations, early detection of disease, and early treatment of disease.

B. Health education - Beginning at an early age, children ought to be taught responsibility for their own health, including good health habits and hygiene, as well as proper nutrition, adequate sleep, and exercise.

VIII. Sexual development

A. Infancy
1. The infant's capacity for sexual response begins early, but infants are too young to be consciously aware of the arousal.
2. Infants begin to discover their bodies during the first year of life.

B. Early childhood - Children are curious about their own bodies, as well as others' bodies.

C. Middle childhood - Sexual experimentation probably increases during these years but becomes more covert because it is less accepted by society.

D. Parents as sex educators - Adolescents whose parents communicated openly with them about sexuality when they were young feel much more comfortable discussing sexual topics with their parents and are more likely to make personal decisions about sexual behavior that reflect parental values and morals.

E. Goals of sex education
1. Help children understand their physical development, prepare for pubertal changes, and accept their own sexuality.
2. Help children understand the great wonders of life.
3. Encourage mature, responsible, and knowledgeable sexual conduct.

IX. Sexual abuse of children

A. Patterns of activity
1. Sexual abuse may include a variety of activities.
2. Molestation is most likely to take place in the child's own home or in that of the molester. Usually the molester is a family member or a friend of the family.
3. The more involved the children become, the more they feel trapped.

B. Effects
1. Victims describe feelings of powerlessness, anger, depression, and anxiety. Low self-esteem is expressed through self-blame, shame, and guilt.
2. Sexual abuse may be a causative factor in some of the most severe mental disorders.
3. Sexual abuse survivors have high levels of anxiety, depression, self-destructive suicidal tendencies, and difficulty with intimate relationships. Depression is the most common symptom.

LEARNING OBJECTIVES/STUDY QUESTIONS

After reading this chapter, you should be able to:

1. Describe how growth proceeds from birth to adolescence, and what factors may create individual differences.

2. Explain the principles of cephalocaudal and proximodistal growth:

    a. Cephalocaudal principle -

    b. Proximodistal principle -

3. Describe the pattern of growth of three organ systems: lymphoid system, reproductive system, and the central nervous system.

4. Describe some of the changes that take place in the brain over development.

5. Discuss how gross motor skills change over development.

6. Discuss how fine motor skills change over development.

7. Examine the development of handedness.

8. Identify and describe four basic categories of physical handicaps in children:

   a.

   b.

   c.

   d.

9. Describe the development of depth perception, perception of form and motion, and face perception.

10. Discuss factors that affect auditory perception.

11. Discuss the advantages and disadvantages of breast-feeding.

12. Discuss some of the factors responsible for obesity in children.

13. Discuss the consequences of malnutrition.

14. Describe the sleep needs of young children.

15. List things that parents can do to develop regular sleep habits for their children.

16.   List components of proper health supervision of the well child by medical personnel.

17.   Describe how children's sexual development changes over age.

18.   State the goals of sex education.

19.   Examine the problem of sexual abuse of children and its effects on their development.

KEY TERMS

In your own words, provide a definition for each of the following terms:

1.   Cephalocaudal principle_____

_____

2.   Proximodistal principle_____

_____

3. Myelinization_____
_____

4. Cerebral cortex_____
_____

5. Lateralization_____
_____

6. Handedness_____
_____

7. Otitis media_____
_____

8. Cross-modal perception_____
_____

9. Gap threshold_____
_____

10. Inanition_____
_____

11. Marasmus_____
_____

12. Kwashiorkor_____
_____

13. Separation anxiety_____
_____

14. Nightmares_____
_____

15. Night terrors_____

16. Sleepwalking_____

APPLICATIONS

For each of the following, fill in the blank with one of the terms listed above.

1. The process by which neurons become coated with an insulating, fatty substance is called **myelinization**.

2. The minimum detectable gap between sounds is called the **gap threshold**.

3. Inanition is also known as **starvation, marasmus in kids**.

4. The ability of a 1-year-old to recognize the visual equivalent of objects that previously have only been touched demonstrates **cross-modal perception**.

5. A 1-year-old who cries a lot when her parents put her down to sleep may be experiencing **separation anxiety**.

6. The preference for using one hand rather than another is called **handedness**.

7. A child who suddenly wakes up in a panic and screams in the middle of the night is experiencing **night terrors**.

8. The largest structure of the forebrain, the **cerebral cortex**, is divided into two hemispheres and controls higher order functions.

9. According to the **proximodistal** principle, large-muscle development in the arms precedes small-muscle development in the hands and fingers.

10. According to the **cephalocaudal** principle, the head develops more rapidly than the feet.

11. A young child who has not received an adequate intake of all nutrients may suffer from **marasmus**.

12. The preference for using one side of the body more than the other in performing special tasks is referred to as **lateralization**.

13. A child who has not received foods with adequate protein and who has a protruding belly and flaky skin is suffering from __Kwashiorkor__.

14. The process by which neurons become coated with myelin, which helps to transmit impulses more efficiently, is called __myelinization__

15. Two-year-old Ralph frequently pulls his ears and is fussy due to a middle-ear disease that is associated with mild hearing loss. Ralph suffers from __otitis media__

SELF-TEST MULTIPLE CHOICE QUESTIONS

Circle the best answer for each question.

1. A period of rapid but decelerating growth occurs
    a. during the first year of life.
    b. during the second year of life.
    c. from the first year through puberty.
    d. during the period of time right before puberty.

2. The disproportionately large size of infants' heads at birth is an example of what principle of growth?
    a. proximodistal principle
    b. cephalocaudal principle
    c. principle of hierarchical integration
    d. principle of the independence of systems

3. At birth, the brain is 25 percent of adult size; at 1 year it is __33%__ of adult size.
    a. 33 percent
    b. 50 percent
    c. 75 percent
    d. 90 percent

4. Which of the following is the correct sequence of the proximodistal principle of development?
    a. eyes, nose, jaw, neck
    b. head, neck, shoulders, middle trunk
    c. middle trunk, shoulders, neck, head
    d. trunk, arms and legs, hands, fingers and toes

5. At 6 months of age, Alexandra can reach out and grab a toy with her hand, but is unable to pick up a small toy with her finger and thumb until she is 9 months old. This illustrates what developmental principle?
    a. cephalocaudal principle
    b. proximodistal principle
    c. principle of hierarchical integration
    d. principle of independence of systems

107

6. By what age do most children show a preference for use of the right hand?
   a. 2
   b. 4
   c. 6
   d. 7

7. The left cerebral hemisphere
   a. controls the left side of the body.
   b. is specialized for language.
   c. is specialized for music.
   d. is superior in recognizing patterns.

8. The first area of the cortex to mature is the
   a. association area.
   b. sensory area.
   c. motor area.
   d. language area.

9. A person who had an injury to Wernicke's area would most likely not be able to
   a. speak.
   b. understand what other people were saying.
   c. recognize other people.
   d. remember what had happened during the accident.

10. What is the correct sequence of motor development in average infants?
    a. reach and miss, sit alone, creep, climb stairs, stand alone
    b. creep, sit alone, climb stairs, stand alone, reach and miss
    c. creep, sit alone, climb stairs, reach and miss, stand alone
    d. sit alone, creep, climb stairs, reach and miss, stand alone

11. Haley can skip smoothly, hop on one foot a distance of 16 feet, and can walk a balance beam. How old is she?
    a. 2
    b. 3
    c. 4
    d. 5

12. Three-month-old Rachel cannot remain seated upright without support. At what age will she acquire this ability?
    a. 6 months
    b. 9 months
    c. 12 months
    d. 14 months

13. A child who was just starting to reach for objects placed in front of him would probably be around
    a. 1 month old.
    b. 4 months old. ✓
    c. 7 months old.
    d. 9 months old.

14. Body weight that is ___20___ percent over what is shown in standard height-weight tables is considered obesity.
    a. 5
    b. 10
    c. 20 ✓
    d. 33

15. Which of the following is an example of a fine motor skill achieved by preschool-aged children?
    a. being able to alternate feet
    b. walking on a balance beam
    c. holding a glass with one hand ✓
    d. balancing on one foot

16. Sex differences found for physical skills before puberty are most likely due to
    a. boys being bigger and stronger than girls.
    b. boys having quicker reaction times.
    c. girls being more mature.
    d. differential expectations of boys and girls. ✓

17. Which of the following is the best statement concerning the physical fitness of children today as compared to children in the 1960s?
    a. Children today are less physically fit. ✓
    b. Children today have greater muscle strength.
    c. Children today have greater physical endurance.
    d. Children today have less body fat.

18. What is the most common physical handicap in children?
    a. speech handicaps ✓
    b. hearing impairments
    c. visual impairments
    d. orthopedic handicaps

19. A child who is 18 months old is asked by her pediatrician to point to various simple objects and body parts in response to tape-recorded names of objects. The doctor controls the volume that each word is spoken. This doctor is testing
    a. the speech reception threshold. ✓
    b. the gap threshold.
    c. sound localization.
    d. expressive language.

20. Little Johnny was able to recognize a stuffed lion toy by feeling it, even though he had previously only seen it and not had the opportunity to touch it. This is an example of
    a. binocular vision.
    b. cross-modal perception.
    c. visual localization.
    d. unilateral perception.

21. One of the advantages that breast-feeding has over bottle-feeding is that
    a. it allows the father to participate more in the feedings.
    b. it is less painful for the mother.
    c. it is assured that no unwanted chemicals will be passed to the baby.
    d. antibodies that immunize the baby from disease are passed from the mother to the baby.

22. One-year-old Tyrone has suffered from malnutrition since birth due to an impoverished environment, and as a result, he has stopped growing. What disease does he have?
    a. anemia
    b. marasmus
    c. choline deficiency
    d. kwashiorkor

23. Which of the following is the best statement regarding getting enough sleep?
    a. Young infants only need about 10 hours of sleep per day, and this amount increases over the first year.
    b. Two-year-olds are more likely to get the amount of sleep they need than are infants.
    c. Infants are more likely to get the amount of sleep they need than are 2-year olds.
    d. Infants are more likely than older children to follow a sleeping schedule.

24. During middle childhood, sexual experimentation may _____ and it also becomes more _____.
    a. decrease; covert
    b. decrease; overt
    c. increase; covert
    d. increase; overt

25. An adult who sexually abuses a child
    a. is most likely a stranger to the child.
    b. is most likely known to the child.
    c. most likely will do it in a place with which the child is not familiar.
    d. most likely will do it in an outdoor setting.

THINKING CRITICALLY ABOUT YOUR DEVELOPMENT

Integrate material from the chapter with your own developmental experiences to respond to the following items.

1. Review the goals of sex education as stated in the text, and then describe the formal sex education you received. Did your education meet these goals? What role do you think parents should have as educators?

2. According to the text, there are wide individual differences in growth patterns for children from birth to age 14 due to heredity, nutrition, education, and other factors. Describe your own growth pattern. How did your growth differ from others in your class? Do you have any theories for those individual differences?

3. The text explains the 1975 federal law which requires that children with disabilities be mainstreamed if possible. Have you attended classes with students with disabilities? If so, how well did you think this federal law worked in practice? Whether you have or not, how do you think this law should be changed, if at all?

4. Are you left-handed or right-handed? Do you always show the same handedness, or do you have some right-handed and left-handed tasks? What does your handedness tell you about your cerebral hemisphere specialization?

5. Think back to your elementary school years. What type of motor skills did you excel in during first or second grade? What type of motor tasks did you enjoy in sixth or seventh grade? Do the two sets of motor skills differ, and if so, how?

ANSWER KEY

APPLICATIONS

1. myelinization
2. gap threshold
3. inanition
4. cross-modal perception
5. separation anxiety
6. handedness
7. night terrors
8. cerebral cortex
9. proximodistal
10. cephalocaudal
11. marasmus
12. lateralization
13. kwashiorkor
14. myelinization
15. otitis media

MULTIPLE CHOICE

1.	a	6.	b	11.	d	16.	d	21.	d
2.	b	7.	b	12.	a	17.	a	22.	b
3.	a	8.	c	13.	b	18.	a	23.	c
4.	d	9.	b	14.	c	19.	a	24.	c
5.	b	10.	a	15.	c	20.	b	25.	b

Chapter 7
COGNITIVE DEVELOPMENT

CHAPTER OUTLINE & OVERVIEW

I. Language

   A. Language and communication - Human infants can communicate through reflexive actions and nonverbal body language.

   B. Elements and rules of language
      1. A phoneme is the smallest unit of sound in a language.
      2. A morpheme is the smallest unit of meaning in a language.
      3. Syntax refers to the grammatical rules of a language.
      4. Semantics deals with the meanings of words and sentences.
      5. Pragmatics refers to the practical use of language to communicate with others in a variety of social contexts.

   C. Theories of language development
      1. Biological theory - According to the nativist view, children inherit a predisposition to learn language at a certain age.
      2. Learning theory - Language is learned just as other behavior is learned: through imitation, conditioning, association, and reinforcement.
      3. Cognitive theory - Language develops out of mental images, and is a direct result of cognitive development.
      4. Interactionist theory - Maturation and experience are both emphasized.

   D. Influences on language development - Both biological maturation and environmental influences affect language development.

   E. Sequence of language development
      1. Prelinguistic period - Children all over the world follow the same timetable and sequence of language development. Babbling begins at 6 months of age.
      2. Inner speech – Private speech helps preschoolers to think.
      3. First spoken words - At about 10 months, infants use holophrases, and by 18 months, may know between 3 to 50 words, mostly referring to objects.
      4. Two-word utterances - Duos usually begin between 18-24 months.
      5. Telegraphic speech - Consists of utterances which exclude unnecessary words. By 30 months of age, children are using 3- to 5-word phrases.
      6. Sentences - By 2 1/2 to 4 years of age, children use multiple-word sentences, and by 6-7 years, children's speech resembles that of adults.

   F. Vocabulary and semantics - Vocabulary grows from about 50 words at age 2 to between 8,000 and 14,000 at age 6. By 18 months, children are able to categorize objects.

114

G. Grammar - Children show some knowledge of grammar by the time they begin using sentences.

H. Pragmatics - the practical ability to use language to communicate with others in a variety of social contexts, it develops during the elementary school years.

I. Gender and communication patterns - Boys' use of language emphasizes dominance, whereas girls emphasize cooperation. Gender differences in interpersonal style have been observed in children as young as 3 years of age.

J. Bilingualism
   1. One half of the world's population is bilingual.
   2. For some children in groups where their first language is a minority language, a second language may be a subtractive influence.
   3. For children whose first language is the majority language, learning a second language is largely an additive experience.
   4. Instruction for minority group children should be primarily in the minority language, with English learned as the second language.

K. Learning to read
   1. Approaches to teaching reading
      a. The skills approach is a method of teaching reading that involves either a phonics approach or a word recognition approach.
      b. The whole-language approach is a method of teaching reading that presents reading materials as a whole so the child learns the meaning of the passage before learning individual words.

II. Approaches to the study of cognition

A. The Piagetian approach emphasizes the qualitative changes in the ways children think.

B. The information-processing approach examines the progressive steps, actions, and operations that take place when the child receives, perceives, remembers, thinks about, and utilizes information.

C. The psychometric approach measures quantitative changes in children's intelligence.

III. A Piagetian perspective - Piaget described four stages of cognitive development:

    A. Sensorimotor stage (birth to 2 years)
        1. The sensorimotor stage involves learning to respond through motor activity to the stimuli that are presented to the senses; the task is learning to coordinate sensorimotor sequences to solve simple problems. There are six sensorimotor substages:
            a. Stage one (0 to 1 month)—exercising reflexes.
            b. Stage two (1 month to 4 months)—primary circular reactions.
            c. Stage three (4 to 8 months)—secondary circular reactions.
            d. Stage four (8 to 12 months)—purposeful coordination of secondary schemes.
            e. Stage five (12 to 18 months)—tertiary circular reactions.
            f. Stage six (18 to 24 months)—mental solutions.
        2. The development of the concept of object permanence is achieved.
        3. Even very young infants can imitate or copy simple behaviors of others.

    B. Preoperational stage (2 to 7 years) - Children do not think logically, but they can think symbolically.
        1. Symbolic play becomes more frequent throughout this stage.
        2. Four- and five-year-old children have some trouble distinguishing fantasy from reality.
        3. Preoperational children are limited in their thinking in the following ways: use of transductive reasoning, syncretism, egocentrism, animism, lacking understanding living kinds, centration, lack of conservation, limitation in classification, and irreversibility.

    C. Concrete operational stage (7 to 11 years) - Children are better at logical reasoning, but only at a concrete level.
        1. They have difficulty with contrary-to-fact reasoning and fail to test hypotheses.
        2. They can arrange objects into hierarchical classifications and comprehend class inclusion relationships.
        3. They are successful at seriation and conservation tasks.
        4. They can perform combinativity, reversibility, associativity, and identity or nullifiability.

    D. Vygotsky's theory of cognitive and language development
        1. In Vygotsky's views, mental functioning primarily is derived, not from maturation, but from social and cultural influences.
        2. As a result of Vygotsky's influence, psychologists now speak of socially shared cognition, socially distributed cognition, and collective memory.
        3. The zone of proximal development is Vygotsky's term for tasks too difficult for children to master alone that need to be mastered with the guidance and assistance of others.
        4. Vygotsky said that language and thought initially develop independently of each other, but eventually merge.

IV. Information processing - describes the way children obtain information, remember it, retrieve it, and use it in solving problems.

    A. Stimuli - Research has shown the importance of stimulation in the learning process.

    B. Habituation - When infants get used to a sound or sight, it loses its novelty and the infants lose interest in it.

    C. Selective attention – Children attend selectively to stimuli, with dramatic increases in selectivity with age.

    D. Memory - the ability to remember is basic to all learning.
        1. Infant memory - Newborns have some memory ability, but it is very short-lived, and early memories are not permanent.
        2. Memory capacity and storage - The process of remembering involves a series of steps. The three-stage model includes:
            a. sensory storage.
            b. short-term storage.
            c. long-term storage.
        3. Metamemory - consists of knowledge of memory strategies that people employ to learn and remember information, which increase from preschool through adolescence.

V. Intelligence - the psychometric approach

    A. Views of intelligence
        1. Binet - Intelligence is a general capacity for comprehension, reasoning, judgment, and memory. It is described in terms of mental age.
        2. Spearman - Besides a general intellectual factor ("g"), there are also specific abilities.
        3. Thurstone - Even though persons are intelligent in one area, they are not necessarily intelligent in other areas. Thurstone identified seven primary mental abilities.
        4. Guilford - The idea of specific abilities was expanded by identifying 120 factors in intelligence.
        5. Gardner - Intelligence is divided into seven dimensions; independence exists for different intelligences in the human neural system.
        6. Sternberg - His triarchic theory of intelligence includes componential, experiential, and contextual intelligence.
        7. Cattell - He described crystallized and fluid dimensions of intelligence.

    B. Intelligence tests
        1. Stanford-Binet – The fourth edition of the Stanford-Binet was published in 1985 and yields scores in four areas: verbal reasoning, quantitative reasoning, abstract/visual reasoning, and short-term memory.

2. The Wechsler Scales – The Wechsler Scales yield a composite IQ score, plus a verbal IQ from the six verbal subscales, and a performance IQ from the six performance subscales.

C. Critique of IQ and IQ tests
1. IQ, school performance, job and personal success - IQ tests do a pretty good job of predicting school performance. Future school success is better predicted by past and present school success than by IQ. IQ tests are more predictive of job success in some occupations than they are in others.
2. Stability of IQ - At age 2, tests cannot predict later scores, but by age 5, future scores are more predictable. However, there are wide variations in patterns even after this age.
3. Personal factors influencing test results - Test results can be influenced by test anxiety, interest in the tasks, and rapport with the test giver.
4. Cultural bias - The major criticism of IQ tests is that they are culturally biased in favor of white, middle-class children.

D. IQ and race - Differences in IQ scores between races are due to social class differences and cultural biases of the tests.

E. Infant intelligence and measurement
1. Developmental quotient (DQ) – The DQ is a score developed by Gesell to evaluate an infant's behavioral level in four categories: motor, language, adaptive, and personal-social.
2. Bayley's Scales of Infant Development – The Bayley Scales assess the developmental status of children from 2 months to 2 ½ years of age in three areas: mental abilities, motor abilities, and infant behavior record.
3. Recent studies – The most recent studies indicate there is more stability in early intelligence than previously thought.

F. Early intervention - High quality programs for economically deprived children can have lasting and valuable effects.

G. Environmental input and cognitive growth – Overall, the environmental influence from parents and school significantly affect cognitive growth.

H. Mental retardation - Mental retardation may be genetically or environmentally determined. Mentally retarded individuals may be classified as borderline, mildly retarded, moderately retarded, severely retarded, or profoundly retarded.

I. High cognitive ability
1. The talent view holds that genetically mediated abilities determine ultimate performance. Genetic influences are partly responsible for high cognitive ability.

2. The character ethic view holds that high cognitive ability is not simply a matter of genetically endowed individuals' rising to high levels of cognitive performance; rather, innate talent must also be nurtured by environments that foster perseverance, hard work, single-mindedness, and goal orientation.
3. The skill acquisition view holds that genetic influence is immaterial to the development of high cognitive ability, which is due to environmental influences. Instead, perseverance, hard work, and single-mindedness enable a person to reach high levels of performance regardless of genetic factors.

VI. School

A. Early childhood education - Some of the different types of programs include: nursery schools, Montessori schools, group-care homes, and day-care centers.

B. Instructional approaches - Compared with children in child-centered programs, children in didactic programs rated their abilities significantly lower, had lower expectations for success on academic tasks, showed more dependency on adults for permission and approval, showed less pride in their accomplishments, and claimed that they worried more about school.

C. American education – Periodically, there are outcries that the American education system is in trouble.

D. Successful schools - Successful schools in the United States emphasize academic excellence, pay attention to the needs of individual students, emphasize no-nonsense discipline, and employ great teachers.

E. Achievement
1. Heredity – Success is not inherited, but heredity is an important factor in intelligence, and intelligence is an important factor in achievement.
2. Learning disabilities - Children with learning disabilities have average or above average general intelligence but manifest specific problems with reading, arithmetic, spelling, and written expression.
3. Achievement motivation – Some children seem to be born with the desire to succeed; others are more laid back and seem not to care. However, part of achievement motivation is instilled in children by parents, teachers, or other influential persons.
4. Dysfunctional family relationships and divorce – Dysfunctional family relationships have a negative effect on school achievement. Divorce itself is perceived as a negative event that can stimulate painful emotions, confusion, and uncertainty in children.
5. One-parent families – Projections show that nearly 60 percent of all children born in 1986 may be expected to spend a large part of a year or longer in a one-parent family before reaching the age of 18.

6. Sociocultural influences – In many instances, socioeconomic status is a better predictor of achievement than race.

LEARNING OBJECTIVES/STUDY QUESTIONS

After reading this chapter, you should be able to:

1. Describe the five basic elements of language:

    a.

    b.

    c.

    d.

    e.

2. Discuss the following theories of language development:

    a. Biological theory -

    b. Learning theory -

    c. Cognitive theory -

    d. Interactionist theory -

3. Briefly discuss both the biological and environmental influences on language development.

4. Briefly summarize the sequence of language development from early infancy through early childhood.

5. Briefly discuss the development of vocabulary, grammar, and pragmatics.

6. Describe gender differences in communication patterns.

7. Discuss the effects of learning a second language on language development.

8. Compare two approaches to teaching reading.

9. Describe Piaget's first three stages of cognitive development, including what children can and cannot do during these stages:

   a.

   b.

   c.

10. Discuss Vygotsky's view of cognitive and language development.

11. Describe some of the factors which are important in the information-processing approach.

12. Identify and describe three stages of memory:

   a.

   b.

   c.

13. Define metamemory and describe some mnemonic strategies.

14. Discuss some of the different definitions or views of intelligence.

15. Discuss measures used for measuring IQ for infants and for children. Provide a critique of how effective and fair these measures are.

16. Identify and describe the five categories of mental retardation:

    a.

    b.

    c.

    d.

    e.

17. Describe some of the different types of early childhood education programs.

18. Discuss the status of the American education system, including a description of successful schools.

19. Describe factors that influence achievement.

KEY TERMS I

In your own words, provide a definition for each of the following terms:

1. Phoneme_____

_____

2. Morpheme_____

_____

3. Syntax_____

_____

4. Semantics_____

_____

5. Pragmatics_____

_____

6. Language acquisition device_____

_____

7. Nativist view _____
_____

8. Cooing _____
_____

9. Babbling _____
_____

10. Holophrases _____
_____

11. Motherese _____
_____

12. Duos _____
_____

13. Telegraphic speech _____
_____

14. Grammar _____
_____

15. Skills approach _____
_____

16. Whole-language approach _____
_____

17. Phonics approach _____
_____

18. Word recognition approach _____
_____

19. Piagetian approach _____
_____

20. Information-processing approach _____
_____

21. Psychometric approach _____
_____

22. Object permanence _____
_____

23. Imitation _____
_____

24. Deferred imitation _____
_____

25. Symbolic play _____
_____

26. Transductive reasoning _____
_____

27. Inductive reasoning _____
_____

28. Deductive reasoning _____
_____

29. Syncretism _____
_____

30. Egocentrism _____
_____

31. Animism _____

_____

32. Centration _____

_____

33. Conservation _____

_____

APPLICATIONS I

For each of the following, fill in the blank with one of the terms listed above.

1. In Noam Chomsky's theory, the _____ refers to the inherited characteristics that allow children to acquire language.

2. In a high-pitched, slower voice, Mary asks her son, "Do you see the ball?" as she presents a red ball to him. Mary's speech is called _____.

3. Sarah teaches reading to second-graders by presenting reading materials as a whole so the children learn the meaning of the passage before learning individual words. Sarah used the _____ approach to teaching reading.

4. A child who says, "Mommy went bye-bye" rather than "Went bye-bye Mommy" is showing some knowledge of _____.

5. Two-word utterances are referred to as _____.

6. When an infant actively seeks out a ball that rolls under a chair and is out of sight, she has achieved _____.

7. A three-month-old who squeals and gurgles is _____.

8. "Kitty drink milk" is an example of _____ speech.

9. A _____ is the smallest unit of sound in a language.

10. A seven-month-old who repeats the syllable "ma-ma-ma" over and over is _____.

11. The tendency to focus on only one aspect of a situation and to ignore the other aspects is called _____.

12. The last time Joe's father was away on a business trip, he returned with a suntan. Now, whenever his father is away on business, Joe mistakenly expects his father to have a tan when he returns. Joe is engaging in _____.

13. A child is shown two balls of clay of the same size. Then one ball is flattened out and the child is asked which of the two is bigger. This is an example of a _____ task.

14. A child who pretends that she and her dog are on a ship that is sailing far away is engaging in _____.

15. A child who knows that dogs bark, and then sees a new dog in her neighborhood and reasons that this dog will also bark, is engaging in _____ reasoning.

KEY TERMS II

In your own words, provide a definition for each of the following terms:

1. Classification_____

2. Irreversibility_____

3. Hierarchical classification_____

4. Class inclusion relationships_____

5. Serialization_____

6. Combinativity_____

7. Reversibility_____

8. Associativity _____
_____

9. Identity or nullifiability _____
_____

10. Zone of proximal development _____
_____

11. Habituation _____
_____

12. Infantile amnesia _____
_____

13. Sensory storage _____
_____

14. Short-term storage _____
_____

15. Long-term storage _____
_____

16. Recall _____
_____

17. Recognition _____
_____

18. Metamemory _____
_____

19. Mnemonic _____
_____

20. Chunking _____
   _____

21. Method of loci _____
   _____

22. Mental age (MA) _____
   _____

23. Chronological age (CA) _____
   _____

24. Intelligence quotient _____
   _____

25. Two-factor theory of intelligence _____
   _____

26. Primary mental abilities _____
   _____

27. Triarchic theory of intelligence _____
   _____

28. Crystallized intelligence _____
   _____

29. Fluid intelligence _____
   _____

30. Developmental quotient (DQ) _____
   _____

31. Mental retardation _____
   _____

32. Learning disabilities_____

_____

33. Dyslexia_____

_____

APPLICATIONS II

For each of the following, fill in the blank with one of the terms listed above.

1. Remembering without cues refers to _____, whereas remembering after cues have been given refers to _____.

2. The tendency to adapt to a repeated stimulus and to lose interest in it is called _____.

3. The _____ is Vygotsky's term for tasks too difficult for children to master alone that need to be mastered with the guidance and assistance of others.

4. A child who understands that all the boys in her class and all the girls in her class equals all of the children in her class understands the operation of _____.

5. A child who understands that if he is given two apples and then those two apples are taken away, he won't have any, understands the operation of _____.

6. A child who says, "That flower wants me to pick it," is engaging in _____.

7. A child who takes all the almonds out of a bowl of mixed nuts and puts them in one pile, and then takes the walnuts and puts them into another pile, demonstrates understanding of _____.

8. The capacity of _____ is about seven digits.

9. Mary has an IQ of 110, but she has a lot of trouble learning simple mathematics. She may have a _____ disability.

10. People often use _____ strategies, such as repeating information, to remember things.

11. The inability of adults to remember events in their lives that took place before they were three years old is called _____.

12. According to Cattell, _____ intelligence is a person's ability to think and reason abstractly.

13. Knowing how it was that you remembered something is part of _____.

14. A child with an average IQ who reads letters from right to left and reads the letter "b" as a "d" may have _____.

15. A child who remembers what furniture is in her house by mentally walking through the different rooms is using the strategy of the _____ to aid in retrieval.

SELF-TEST MULTIPLE CHOICE QUESTIONS

Circle the best answer for each question.

1. When a child learns to speak quietly in certain places, such as a church service or a library, she has learned about a language rule pertaining to
    a. semantics.
    b. syntax.
    c. phonology.
    d. pragmatics.

2. According to Chomsky, children are born with inherited characteristics that enable them to listen to and imitate speech sounds and patterns called the
    a. language deficit.
    b. language acquisition device.
    c. autobiographical memory.
    d. zone of proximal development.

3. The smallest unit of sound in a language defines
    a. phonemes.
    b. vowels.
    c. morphemes.
    d. syllables.

4. Six-month-old Beth repeats the same sound over and over, "baa-baa-baa-baa." This form of language is called
    a. vocables.
    b. babbling.
    c. holophrastic speech.
    d. telegraphic speech.

5. When one-year-old Desiree raises both arms and says to her mother, "Mama!" her mother understands that Desiree is trying to convey "Mama, pick me up!" This demonstrates
	a. a duo.
	b. expressive jargon.
	c. a holophrase.
	d. telegraphic speech.

6. One-year-old Andre says "juice" when he wants to drink juice as well as when he wants anything to drink. His one-word utterance illustrates
	a. egocentric speech.
	b. infant-directed speech.
	c. telegraphic speech.
	d. holophrastic speech.

7. What is the first stage of sensorimotor intelligence?
	a. mental solutions
	b. exercising reflexes
	c. primary circular reactions
	d. tertiary circular reactions

8. Which of the following illustrates telegraphic speech?
	a. "Mama work."
	b. "Up!"
	c. "Did Daddy goes to the store?"
	d. "Baa-baa-baa-baa."

9. Robin adheres to the whole-language approach to literacy, in which all language processes are studied
	a. as a series of facts.
	b. bilingually.
	c. using "chunking" to facilitate language acquisition.
	d. in a natural context.

10. After many car rides with her parents, 18-month-old Susan pretends that she is driving a car. This ability to pretend is called
	a. cross-modal transference.
	b. visual-recognition memory.
	c. object permanence.
	d. deferred imitation.

11. Four-year-old Rose views everything in relation to herself. Her self-centered view is called
	a. animism.
	b. centration.
	c. irreversibility.
	d. egocentrism.

12. When 9-year-old Nathan's mother blew up an inflatable beach ball, he understood that if he let the air out, it would return to its original form. Nathan understands
    a. decentering.
    b. reversibility.
    c. transformation.
    d. seriation.

13. A child is presented with two identical balls of clay. As the child watches, one ball is rolled into a sausage, while the other remains untouched. The child is asked which has more clay, the sausage shape or the untouched ball of clay. This is a classic experiment of conservation of
    a. area.
    b. substance.
    c. volume.
    d. number.

14. Object permanence is achieved during what stage of cognitive development?
    a. sensorimotor stage
    b. formal operational stage
    c. preoperational stage
    d. concrete operational stage

15. What theory of language development suggests that language is learned just as other behavior is learned: through imitation, conditioning, association, and reinforcement?
    a. cognitive theory
    b. learning theory
    c. interactionist theory
    d. biological theory

16. If you cannot remember the birth of a younger sibling and you were two years old at the time, your lack of memory is called
    a. implicit memory.
    b. infantile amnesia.
    c. visual-recognition memory.
    d. cross-modal transference.

17. Melissa is memorizing her lines for a school play. Her ability to understand that rehearsal is a useful strategy for improving her memory is called
    a. sequencing.
    b. metamemory.
    c. semantic elaboration.
    d. metalinguistic awareness.

18. The IQ score equals
    a. CA/MA x 10.
    b. MA/CA x 100.
    c. MA/CA x 10.
    d. CA/MA x 100.

19. The IQ score takes into account a student's
    a. mental and social age.
    b. social and chronological age.
    c. mental and functional age.
    d. mental and chronological age.

20. The Bayley Scales of Infant Development consists of the following parts, *except*
    a. mental abilities.
    b. motor abilities.
    c. temperament profile.
    d. infant behavior record.

21. Which of the following is **not** a concept in Sternberg's definition of intelligence?
    a. practical intelligence
    b. contextual intelligence
    c. componential intelligence
    d. experiential intelligence

22. What element of Sternberg's triarchic theory of intelligence refers to the ability to adapt to our culture?
    a. performance element
    b. componential element
    c. experiential element
    d. contextual element

23. Tom has acquired knowledge of the law through his 30 years as a litigator and from his years studying in law school. His knowledge, accumulated over the years, is called
    a. fluid intelligence.
    b. mechanical intelligence.
    c. pragmatical intelligence.
    d. crystallized intelligence.

24. Joellyn has an IQ score of 40, and has language and motor delays, requiring close supervision. She is classified with
    a. mild retardation.
    b. moderate retardation.
    c. severe retardation.
    d. profound retardation.

25. When Tony reads, letters appear to be reversed. What is Tony's learning disability?
    a. myopia
    b. dyslexia
    c. dyscalculia
    d. attention-deficit disorder

THINKING CRITICALLY ABOUT YOUR DEVELOPMENT

Integrate material from the chapter with your own developmental experiences to respond to the following items.

1. Identify some mnemonic devices and provide examples of each. What mnemonic devices do you use to study for an exam?

2. Describe the biological and environmental influences on your language development. Be specific and give examples.

3. Achievement motivation is influenced by a number of factors. Identify these influences and relate how each factor has applied to your academic achievement.

4. How are your communication patterns different because of your gender? Be specific and give examples.

5. What grade would you give the public schools you have attended? Which was the best public school you have attended? Why?

ANSWER KEY

APPLICATIONS I

1. language acquisition device
2. motherese
3. whole-language
4. syntax
5. duos
6. object permanence
7. cooing
8. telegraphic
9. phoneme
10. babbling
11. centration
12. syncretism
13. conservation
14. symbolic play
15. deductive reasoning

APPLICATIONS II

1. recall, recognition
2. habituation
3. zone of proximal development
4. combinativity
5. identity or nullifiability
6. animism
7. classification
8. short-term storage
9. learning
10. mnemonic
11. infantile amnesia
12. fluid
13. metamemory
14. dyslexia
15. method of loci

MULTIPLE CHOICE

1. d
2. b
3. a
4. b
5. c
6. d
7. b
8. a
9. d
10. d
11. d
12. b
13. b
14. a
15. b
16. b
17. b
18. b
19. d
20. c
21. a
22. d
23. d
24. b
25. b

Chapter 8
EMOTIONAL DEVELOPMENT

CHAPTER OUTLINE & OVERVIEW

I. Attachment

    A. Meaning and importance
   1. Attachment is the feeling that binds a child to a parent or caregiver.
   2. All infants need to form a secure emotional attachment to someone.
   3. The formation of attachment is important to children's total development.

    B. Multiple attachments
   1. Children can form close attachments to more than one person.
   2. Because children can form multiple attachments does not mean that caregivers can be constantly changed.
   3. The important factor in attachment development is the total dialogue that goes on between parent and child.

    C. Specific attachments - Attachments to specific persons do not develop until about 6 or 7 months of age.
   1. Maturation - Before attachment can occur, infants must learn to distinguish humans from inanimate objects, to distinguish between different people, and to develop a specific attachment to one person.
   2. Decreases in attachment behavior - Specific attachments are at their maximum from 12 to 18 months, and then attachment behaviors decrease over the course of the second year.

    D. Nonattached children and insecure attachment
   1. Nonattached children may make no distinction between their own parents and other adults.
   2. Insecurely attached children, particularly girls, can be excessively dependent on their parents. Insecure boys may show aggressive and attention-seeking behaviors.

    E. Critique of attachment theory
   1. Attachment theory focuses on maternal rather than on parental attachment.
   2. Attachment theory should also imply that there is an optimal level of care for children in our society. Attachment theorists need to take a more balanced approach toward both the needs of children and the needs of caregivers.

    F. Separation anxiety
   1. Symptoms - Signs of separation anxiety, such as crying when the parent leaves, vary according to individual differences, age, and the frequency and length of separation.

2. Effects of repeated or long-term separation - With long-term separation, children initially protest, then reach a period of despair, followed by detachment and withdrawal. The trauma of extensive separation without an adequate substitute can be quite severe.
3. Age factors - Distress over separation is greatest after 6 months and until about 3 years of age, but even preschool and school age children can be affected.

G. Homesickness - Homesickness is one possible manifestation of separation anxiety.

H. Reunion behavior - Some children become very dependent and possessive; others may become angry.

I. Strangers - Fear of strangers ordinarily begins at about 6 or 7 months of age and increases until about 2 years, after which it declines.

J. Baby-sitters and substitute caregivers - The question of the long-term effects of substitute care on children is a very controversial one. The quality of the care is an important factor; high-quality daycare can have positive effects.

II. Development of trust and security

A. Theoretical perspectives
1. Erikson suggested that the core of personality is formed in infancy as infants learn basic trust.
2. Margaret Mahler emphasized the importance of the mother-child relationship.

B. Requirements for the development of trust and security in infants.
1. Children should receive regular and adequate feedings.
2. Babies need to get sufficient sucking.
3. Children need to experience cuddling, and physical contact.
4. The most important requirement for the development of trust and security in children is for parents to show them that they love them.

C. Some causes of distrust and insecurity:
1. Parental deprivation - The longer the deprivation, the more pronounced the effects.
2. Tension - Being cared for by anxious parents can lead to emotional insecurity.
3. Exposure to frightening experiences may lead to insecurity if it is traumatic.
4. Frequent disapproval and criticism may make children unsure of themselves.
5. Children who are overprotected may become anxious.

6. Children who are overindulged may not be prepared for dealing with frustrations later in life.

III. Development of emotions

A. Components - Emotions involve the basic components of stimuli, feelings, physiological arousal, and behavioral response.

B. Functions - Emotions are adaptive, are a means of communication, and are important in social relationships and sociomoral development. They are powerful motivators, as well as a source of pleasure or of pain.

C. Basic emotions
1. The basic emotions which can be recognized by people all over the world are: happiness, sadness, anger, surprise, disgust, and fear.
2. The ability to interpret correctly the emotions and feelings of others is important in interpersonal relationships.

D. Timetable of development - Izard claims that emotions develop according to a biological timetable, but others suggest that all emotions can be experienced at birth.

E. Children's fears - Children are not born afraid, except for two fears: fear of loud noises and fear of falling. Yet, beginning about the first year of life, they develop fears, some through actual experiences or because of limited understanding.

F. Children's worries - One study found the three most common areas of worry reported by children concerned school, health, and personal harm.

G. Environmental and biological influences in development - Emotional responses are partly learned but also have a biological component. Emotional expression and behavior in infancy tell us something about the personality of the child later in life.

H. Aggression - Aggression in children takes two forms: verbal or physical. Aggressive behavior in children often has its origins in the family situation. The consequences of early aggression result in low academic achievement, early school dropout, heavy drug use, and juvenile delinquency.

I. Emotional expression and control - To be an emotionally mature individual means to develop proper balance between emotional expression and control. The goal is to help children move from external authority to internal control Children who are exposed to high levels of parental positive affect are the ones who become most socialized and most cooperative.

IV. Differences in temperament

    A. Personality and temperament
        1. Personality is the sum total of the physical, mental, emotional, and social characteristics of an individual; it is a global concept that is not static.
        2. Temperament refers to relatively consistent, basic dispositions inherent in people, which influence their behavior. Temperament is composed primarily of inherited biological factors; however, as development proceeds, the expression of temperament becomes increasingly influenced by environmental factors.

    B. Components and patterns of temperament
        1. Buss and Plomin specify three traits as constituting temperament: emotionality, activity, and sociability.
        2. Thomas and Chess specify nine components of temperament: rhythmicity, activity level, approach/withdrawal, adaptability, sensory threshold, mood, intensity of mood expression, distractibility, and persistence. They found three temperament patterns: easy, difficult, and slow-to-warm-up.

    C. Stability of temperament
        1. One study assessed the relationships between early temperament and behavioral problems across 12 years. Long-term continuity of individual differences was apparent for both sexes. Boys and girls who were characterized by lack of control in early childhood were more likely to experience behavioral problems a decade later.

V. Development of self, autonomy, self-concept, and self-esteem

    A. Self-awareness - Children begin to understand their separateness from others and other things.

    B. Autonomy – Erikson said that the chief psychosocial task between 1 and 2 years of age is the development of autonomy. As the self emerges, children begin to want some independence.

    C. Separation-individuation - According to Mahler, at about 5 months until about 3 years, a period of separation-individuation occurs during which the infant gradually develops a self apart from the mother.

    D. Self-definition and self-concept - By 3 years, children describe themselves in exaggerated and positive terms, but by the middle elementary school years, their descriptions become more realistic.

E. Self-reference and self-efficacy
1. Self-reference has to do with ourselves, our estimates of our abilities, and how capable and effective we are in dealing with others and the world. Estimates of our effectiveness have been termed self-efficacy.
2. Bandura suggested that children's judgment of self-efficacy stems from personal accomplishments, their comparisons to others, persuasion, and the person's arousal level.

F. Self-esteem - How children feel about themselves is their self-esteem. There are four primary sources of self-esteem: children's emotional relationship with parents, their social competence with peers, their intellectual abilities, and the attitudes of society toward them.

G. Conclusions – How children feel about themselves is crucial to their mental health, as well as to their later relationships and successes in life.

LEARNING OBJECTIVES/STUDY QUESTIONS

After reading this chapter, you should be able to:

1. Define attachment and describe to whom infants can become attached.

2. Describe nonattached and insecurely attached children.

3. Critique attachment theory.

4. Describe symptoms of separation anxiety and discuss the long-term effects of repeated or long-term separation on children.

5. Describe stranger fear and children's reactions to substitute caregivers.

6. List requirements for the development of trust and security in infants.

7. Identify causes of distrust and insecurity.

8. Identify and describe components of emotions and list important functions of emotions.

9. List the basic emotions and describe the timetable of development according to Izard.

10. Describe how children's fears and worries develop.

11. Discuss two forms of aggression in children.

12. Discuss how parents can help or hinder their child in developing balance between emotional expression and control.

13. Distinguish between personality and temperament.

14. Identify and describe the three traits that Buss and Plomin suggest constitute temperament.

   a.

   b.

   c.

15. Identify and define Thomas and Chess' nine components of temperament, and three temperament patterns of children.

16. Describe the development of self-awareness.

17. Discuss the development of autonomy and separation-individuation.

18. Discuss the sources of self-efficacy and self-esteem.

KEY TERMS

In your own words, provide a definition for each of the following terms:

1. Attachment _____
   _____

2. Nonattached children _____
   _____

3. Insecurely attached children _____
   _____

4. Autistic phase _____
   _____

5. Symbiosis _____
   _____

6. Epinephrine _____
   _____

7. Personality _____
   _____

8. Temperament _____
   _____

9. Attention-deficit disorder _____
   _____

10. Separation-individuation _____
    _____

11. Self-reference _____
    _____

12. Self-efficacy _____

_____

13. Self-esteem _____

_____

APPLICATIONS

For each of the following, fill in the blank with one of the terms listed above.

1. The sum total of the physical, mental, social, and emotional characteristics of an individual makes up the _personality_.

2. Starting at 5 months, Haley began to develop a self apart from her mother. This period of _separation/individuation_ will last until about age 3.

3. Sarah is so dependent on her parents that she won't let them out of her sight at all. Sarah's overdependence on her parents is attributed to their personal problems. Sarah is a(n) _insecurely-attached_ child.

4. Whenever Lenny's parents return home, he makes no effort to greet them, nor does he seem to care that they have come home. Lenny may be _nonattached_ to his parents.

5. According to Thomas and Chess, an infant who is on a regular schedule, is generally happy, and adjusts easily to new situations has an easy _temperament_.

6. A child who thinks that he is not intelligent, that people don't like him, and in general, has a very negative impression of his own worth can be said to have low _self-esteem_.

7. A child who runs to his father rather than a stranger when he is upset, and who wants to be held and talked to has developed a specific _attachment_ to his father.

8. Eddie is excessively active, has great difficulty concentrating for any length of time in school, and often jumps out of his seat. Eddie may have _attention-deficit disorder_.

9. According to Mahler, a 1-month-old baby who believes that her mother exists to satisfy her basic needs is in the _autistic_ phase.

10. According to Mahler, when an infant has established dependency on his mother, he is in the phase of _symbiosis_.

11. A hormone secreted by the adrenal glands that produces physiological arousal is called __epinephrine__

12. Our perceptions of our actual skill and personal effectiveness refers to __self-efficacy__

13. Estimates of our abilities of how effectively we deal with others and the world defines __self-reference__

SELF-TEST MULTIPLE CHOICE QUESTIONS

Circle the best answer for each question.

1. The feeling that binds a person and a child together is called
   a. empathy.
   b. imprinting.
   c. attachment.
   d. synchrony.

2. The sequence of developing attachments is from
   a. people in general to specific individuals.
   b. specific individuals to people in general.
   c. multiple attachments to single attachments.
   d. single attachments to multiple attachments.

3. Lori gave birth to twins and began developing a loving emotional bond with them immediately. This bond that forms is called
   a. empathy.
   b. temperament.
   c. attachment.
   d. imprinting.

4. Attachment behaviors are at their peak
   a. before 6 months of age.
   b. from 6 to 12 months of age.
   c. from 12 to 18 months of age.
   d. during the third year.

5. A child who constantly cries to be picked up and then continues to cry when he is held, and generally is very clingy to his parents may be
   a. nonattached.
   b. insecurely attached.
   c. precocious.
   d. multiply attached.

6. Research on gender differences in insecurely attached preschool children (Turner, 1991) found that insecure girls showed more _____ behavior than secure girls.
   a. dependent
   b. controlling
   c. assertive
   d. attention-seeking

7. A child who is separated for a long time from her parents will likely go through which of the following sequences of phases?
   a. protest, despair, detachment
   b. despair, detachment, protest
   c. protest, detachment, despair
   d. despair, protest, detachment

8. A six-year-old boy presents three major symptoms: excessive activity, inattentiveness, and impulsivity. What is his diagnosis?
   a. autism
   b. obsessive-compulsive disorder
   c. generalized anxiety disorder
   d. attention-deficit hyperactive disorder

9. Children do not generally exhibit a fear of strangers until after about
   a. 2 months old.
   b. 4 months old.
   c. 6 months old.
   d. 2 years old.

10. Which of the following represents the developmental sequences of emotional expression identified by Izard?
    a. interest, anger, shyness, guilt
    b. anger, shyness, guilt, interest
    c. shyness, guilt, interest, anger
    d. guilt, interest, anger, shyness

11. According to Erik Erikson, the "cornerstone of vital personality" is the development of
    a. symbiosis.
    b. autonomy.
    c. independence.
    d. basic trust.

12. According to Mahler, during what phase do children establish dependency on their mother?
    a. autistic phase
    b. symbiosis phase
    c. basic trust phase
    d. autonomy phase

13. Which of the following is *not* considered to be a function of emotions?
    a. Emotions are adaptive and help ensure survival.
    b. Emotions can indicate when physiological needs such as hunger should be met.
    c. Emotions are a useful means of communication.
    d. Emotions are powerful motivators of development.

14. Which of the following is *not* a basic emotion?
    a. jealousy
    b. surprise
    c. disgust
    d. anger

15. According to Izard, which of the following emotions is present at birth?
    a. joy
    b. anger
    c. sadness
    d. disgust

16. An infant keeps a very regular schedule of hunger, sleep, and excretion. This relates to what dimension of temperament?
    a. adaptability
    b. quality of mood
    c. rhythmicity
    d. threshold of responsiveness

17. The relatively consistent, basic disposition which is inherent in every person that underlies much of our behavior is referred to as
    a. personality.
    b. temperament.
    c. reactivity.
    d. emotionality.

18. Activity level, sensory threshold, and predominant quality of mood are dimensions of
    a. neuroticism.
    b. temperament.
    c. attachment.
    d. sociability.

19. Marco is a very active child with irregular schedules. He is prone to having temper tantrums when he doesn't get what he wants. According to Thomas and Chess, he would be classified as a(n)
    a. easy child.
    b. slow-to-warm-up child.
    c. reactive child.
    d. difficult child.

20. According to Erikson, the major psychological task between 1 and 2 years of age is the development of
    a. trust.
    b. identity.
    c. industry.
    d. autonomy.

21. According to Mahler, the period between 5 months of age until age 3 involves
    a. the development of trust.
    b. the development of separation-individuation.
    c. growing dependency needs.
    d. a fusing of personalities with the mother.

22. Greg did very poorly on a task, but when he is asked how well he will do it the next time, he says that he will do very well. Based on just this information, how old is Greg?
    a. 3 years
    b. 7 years
    c. 9 years
    d. 13 years

23. According to Bandura, the emotional source of self-efficacy refers to
    a. if a child feels badly because he did not do well on a task.
    b. how the child feels in comparison to her peers.
    c. whether the child has been encouraged or discouraged.
    d. the level of physiological arousal which can affect judgments either positively or negatively.

24. Children's emotional relationships with parents, their social competence with peers, their intellectual prowess at school, and the attitudes of society and community toward them are four primary sources of
    a. self-esteem.
    b. self-reference.
    c. self-efficacy.
    d. self-knowledge.

25. At what age does self-awareness begin to develop?
    a. 6 months
    b. 12 months
    c. 18 months
    d. 24 months

THINKING CRITICALLY ABOUT YOUR DEVELOPMENT

Integrate material from the chapter with your own developmental experiences to respond to the following items.

1. Do you recall ever having experienced separation anxiety, homesickness, stranger anxiety, excessive fears or worries?

2. What sources of self-efficacy were particularly important in your life? Why?

3. What sources of self-esteem were particularly important in your life? Why?

4. Evaluate your own temperament using the nine components developed by Thomas and Chess (1977). Which category do you fit into?

5. When you felt threatened or insecure in elementary school, who did you turn to for support or comfort? Who did you turn to in middle school/junior high school? High school? College? How did these people meet your needs?

ANSWER KEY

APPLICATIONS

1. personality
2. separation-individuation
3. insecurely attached
4. nonattached
5. temperament
6. self-esteem
7. attachment
8. attention-deficit disorder
9. autistic
10. symbiosis
11. epinephrine
12. self-efficacy
13. self-reference

MULTIPLE CHOICE

1.	c	6.	a	11.	d	16.	c	21.	b
2.	a	7.	a	12.	b	17.	b	22.	a
3.	c	8.	d	13.	b	18.	b	23.	d
4.	c	9.	c	14.	a	19.	d	24.	a
5.	b	10.	a	15.	d	20.	d	25.	b

Chapter 9
SOCIAL DEVELOPMENT

CHAPTER OUTLINE & OVERVIEW

I. Sociocultural influences - Bronfenbrenner developed an ecological model for understanding social influences. The child is at the center of the model and is surrounded by systems of external influences, which have both positive and negative effects, including: the microsystem, mesosystem, exosystem, and macrosystem.

II. The family and socialization
    A. The family's role
        1. Different types of families exist: single-parent family, nuclear family, extended family, blended or reconstituted family, binuclear family, communal family, gay or lesbian family, and a cohabiting family. Total influence varies with family forms.
        2. Children are socialized initially through the family through formal instruction, rewards and punishment, reciprocal parent-child interaction, and observational modeling.
        3. Not all children are influenced to the same degree by their families, and not all react in the same way to the same environment.

    B. Parental competence and family environment
        1. Parents' psychological adjustment - Parents who are psychologically healthy are more likely to have a positive effect on their children's development.
        2. Marital quality - The quality of the marital relationship affects children's adjustments and development and influences children's behavior problems over a wide age span. Not all marital conflict is harmful to children.

    C. Patterns of parenting
        1. Baumrind has identified three general styles of parenting: authoritarian, permissive, and authoritative. Authoritative parenting works best in the socialization of children.
        2. According to Schaefer, successful parenting shows the maximum amount of love and the right balance between autonomy and control.
        3. Research shows that the one parenting variable that is most related to adjustment is love. Parents who genuinely love their children provide them with the most important requirement for successful socialization.

    D. Discipline
        1. Children respond more readily to parents within the context of a loving, trusting relationship of mutual esteem.
        2. Discipline is more effective when it is consistent rather than erratic.
        3. Learning is enhanced if responses involve rewards and punishments.

4. Discipline is more effective when applied as soon after the offense as possible.
5. Discipline that inflicts pain should not be used.
6. Discipline becomes less effective if it is too strict or too often applied.
7. Extremes of either permissiveness or authoritarianism are counterproductive.
8. All children are different.
9. Discipline needs to take into account children's age.
10. Methods of discipline to be avoided are those that threaten the child's security or development of self-esteem.

E. The father's role - Even when mothers work full-time, many fathers do not participate in household chores to the same extent as do mothers.

F. Working mothers - While studies show that maternal employment is not uniformly detrimental to the child's well-being, neither is it likely that it is uniformly beneficial. When socioeconomic status is taken into account, results show that there is a stronger negative net effect of maternal employment on the child in high socioeconomic status families.

G. Sibling relationships
 1. Birth order
    a. Research indicates that firstborn children have some advantages over other children in the family.
    b. The youngest in the family are also usually given special attention because they are the youngest.
    c. Middle children tend to have lower self-esteem than do firstborn and last born, probably because they have a less well-defined function within the family.
 2. Number of siblings - In general terms, the greater the number of children, the less they will be able to complete their education.
 3. Gender - The sex of a sibling may also be of some significance.
 4. Older brothers and sisters - Having older brothers and sisters in the same family can have a significant influence on younger children--either positively or negatively.

H. Grandparents
 1. The grandparent-grandchild relationship is an important relationship for children for a number of different reasons:
    a. Grandparents can help children feel loved and secure.
    b. Grandparents can help children to know, trust, and understand other people.
    c. Grandparents help children to bridge the gap between the past and the present.
    d. Grandparents can provide children with experiences and supervision that their own parents do not have money or time to provide.

    e. Grandparents—as a result of living—can give children a fine sense of values and a philosophy of life.
    f. Grandparents can give children a wholesome attitude toward old age.
  2. When problems occur with grandparents, they usually arise over one or more of the following problems:
    a. Grandparents are often puzzled about the roles they're expected to play in relationship to their grandchildren.
    b. Grandparents may have different ideas about raising children.
    c. Grandparents have a tendency to give unsolicited advice to parents and grandchildren and to preach.
    d. Sometimes parents become jealous of the affection that the children develop for their grandparents.
    e. Some grandparents become too possessive of their grandchildren.
    f. In the case of disagreements, parents and grandparents need to talk things over.

III. Nonnuclear families

  A. One-parent families
    1. The female-headed family – One of the most important problems of the female-headed family is limited income. Mothers who are left alone to bring up their children themselves may have difficulty performing all family functions well.
    2. The male-headed family – Solo fathers do not suffer poverty to the same extent as do solo mothers, although financial pressure is still one of the most common complaints. Also, most single fathers are concerned about not spending enough time with their children.
    3. Effects of paternal absence on sons - The earlier a boy is separated from his father and the longer the separation is, the more affected the boy will be in his early years.
    Father absence may also affect the development of masculinity. Boys in single-parent families have a lower level of education attainment and consequent lower income as adults. The effect of father absence is dependent partially on whether boys have surrogate male models. Father absence for girls may make it more difficult to relate to the opposite sex. A father-present home is not necessarily always better for the children than a father-absent home.

  B. Gay and lesbian families - An increasing number of gay men and lesbian couples are raising children.

  C. Divorce and children
    1. A growing number of clinicians emphasize that children perceive divorce as a major, negative event that stimulates painful emotions, confusion, and uncertainty.

2. Researchers have found a large number of variables—individual, family, and environmental—that affect the quality of adjustment to divorce.
3. Reactions include: mourning and grief, a heightened sense of insecurity and anxiety, blaming themselves, preoccupation with reconciliation, and anger and resentment.
4. Children have adjustments to make: adjusting to the absence of one parents, and special adjustments are necessary when the parents get emotionally involved with other persons.
5. Custody refers to both legal custody and physical custody.
    a. In sole legal custody, the noncustodial parent forfeits the right to make decisions about the children.
    b. In joint legal custody, custody is shared between the two parents, with parental obligations and rights left as they were during the marriage.
6. Under law, child support is an obligation of both the father and the mother whether the parents are married or not.
7. Visitation rights are given to the parent who was not given custody. These rights may be unlimited or restrictive.
8. Children's well-being is inversely correlated with the level of postdivorce conflict that exists and persists between parents. A new ideal for cooperative postdivorce parenting is coparenting by divorced parents.
9. Two factors that result in the greatest impact on the mother and child are payment of child support and the frequency and emotional quality of the father's relationship with the child.

D. Stepfamilies - There may be problems with stepfamilies because of the following reasons:
1. Stepparents have unrealistically high expectations;
2. Stepparents enter into their new family with guilt and regret over their failed marriage;
3. Stepparents' role is ill-defined;
4. Stepparents must deal with children who have already been socialized by another set of parents;
5. Stepparents often get rejection and criticism;
6. Stepparents are faced with unresolved emotional issues from the prior marriage and divorce;
7. Stepparents must cope with stepsibling feelings and relationships.

E. Foster care - The number of children under foster parent care has skyrocketed, but it is far from an ideal situation.

F. Adoptive families
1. Many adoptive parents also have children of their own.
2. About half of those who petition for adoption are related to the child they wish to adopt.
3. The benefits of open adoptions have been questioned.

G. Adolescent mothers - Adolescent mothers are at greater risk of family instability and negative educational and economic outcomes and their children are more likely to experience problem behavior.

IV. The development of peer relationships

A. Psychosocial development - Children pass through four stages: autosociality, childhood heterosociality, homosociality, and adolescent and adult heterosociality.

B. Infants and toddlers
1. Infants interact with one another from about 5 months, primarily through looking and smiling.
2. By 9 months, they will offer toys and comfort others in distress.
3. By the time they are toddlers, they have learned about how to fend for themselves in a group.

C. Early childhood
1. Two-year-olds will play alongside one another and show some preferences in playmates.
2. By 3 years, more friendly encounters occur, and aggressive behavior gradually declines.
3. By 4 and 5 years, children share affection and objects, and will begin to form larger groups of playmates.

D. Middle childhood
1. Friendships – The older that children become, the more important that companionship with friends becomes.
2. Popularity - Peer acceptance is predictive of later adjustment during adolescence.
3. Peer rejection - Peer relationships within the school setting have a great influence on children's concurrent and later academic, behavioral, and emotional adjustment. Rejected children have been found to be at heightened risk for a number of negative outcomes.
4. Least popular – Children who are considered least popular share several characteristics, such as self-centeredness and emotional disturbance.
5. Conflicts – Conflicts occur more frequently among friends than among nonfriends, and they last longer. They occur more frequently between individuals who are socially interdependent and who interact over substantial periods of time.
6. There is a difference between children who are unliked and those who are disliked.
7. Cruelty and aggression – Bullies' primary motive seems to be to gain control of others as a means of feeling important themselves. There is substantial evidence that a small minority of children are consistently targeted for victimization by their peers.

8. Loneliness – Those children who are rejected and actively disliked by their peers in school report significantly more loneliness than average-accepted and popular children.

E. Social cognition - the capacity to understand social relationships. Selman has described five stages in the development of social role taking:
1. Stage 0 – Egocentric undifferentiated stage (age 0 to 6).
2. Stage 1 – Differentiated or subjective perspective-taking stage (age 6 to 8).
3. Stage 2 – Self-reflective thinking or reciprocal perspective-taking stage (age 8 to 10).
4. Stage 3 – Third-person or mutual perspective-taking stage (age 10 to 12).
5. Stage 4 – In-depth and societal perspective-taking stage (adolescence to adulthood).

F. Family influences - The family plays the primary role in the development of social competence.

V. Television as a socializing influence

A. Viewing habits - Children between the ages of 2 and 11 spend about 22 hours per week watching television.

B. Violence and aggression - Television violence does have an adverse affect on children. The effect is interdependent. Aggressive children select more violent television programs and view more of them, and those who watch more violent programs tend to be more aggressive.

C. Factual versus fictional - During the years from about 3 to 12, children gradually acquire an understanding of the distinctions between real and fictional television content.

D. Family interaction - Extensive viewing has been associated with a decrease in family interaction, social communication, and interpersonal conversation.

E. Cognitive development - Heavy TV viewing by children of low socioeconomic status has been associated with higher scholastic achievement and reading comprehension and at the same time with lower abilities among children of high socioeconomic status.

F. Commercials - Television advertising is influential in both positive and negative ways.

G. Positive effects - Some educational programs, like "Sesame Street," have been shown to have positive benefits. Television can promote good health and nutrition habits and prosocial behavior.

VI. Computers

   A. The Internet – Some 25,000 interconnected networks made up of several hundred thousand host computers in their servers span the globe, ready to exchange information and allow people to connect with others all over the world, resulting in a decentralized network of data shown on thousands of computers that make up the network.

   B. The World Wide Web – The Web was developed in 1992, resulting in an explosion of Internet users.

   C. Inappropriate materials – Parents and lawmakers have sought to install devices in computers that limit the access of children to such materials. Legislation is also proposed to help protect children from these kind of exposures.

   D. Effects – Children now may be the best informed generation ever in the United States; however, there are negative effects.

VII. The development of gender roles

   A. Meaning - Gender refers to our biological sex, whether male or female; and gender roles are outward expressions of masculinity or femininity in social settings.

   B. Influences on gender roles
      1. Biological - Gender development is influenced by the chromosomal combination and by the sex hormones.
      2. Cognitive – Cognitive theory suggests that sex-role identity has its beginning in the gender cognitively assigned to the child at birth and subsequently accepted by him or her while growing up.
      3. Environmental
         a. The child learns sex-typed behavior through rewards and punishment, indoctrination, observation of others, modeling, and limitation.
         b. Giving children gender-specific toys may have considerable influence on vocational choices.
         c. Children also find appropriate sex roles through a process of identification, especially with parents of the same sex.

   C. Age and gender-role development
      1. By age 2, children are aware of boys and girls and sex-typed roles.
      2. By age 3, children choose sex-typed toys although they are unaware why; this changes by age 5.
      3. By age 7, children have developed a sense of gender constancy.

D. Stereotypes - Although standards of maleness and femaleness are undergoing change, there is still much evidence of traditional stereotypes. There are numerous problems with stereotypes.

E. Androgyny - Androgynous persons are not sex-typed with respect to roles, although they are distinctly male or female in gender.

VIII. Moral development

A. Moral judgment - According to Piaget, children move from a morality of constraint to a morality of cooperation, from heteronomy to autonomy in making moral judgments, and from expiatory punishment to punishment of reciprocity.

B. Moral behavior - Moral behavior is affected by moral motivation and moral inhibition. Over time, children come to depend more on internal than external factors when determining what is right and wrong.

C. Conscience development - Conscience development is the process of internalization of values. Age 3 is a developmental landmark in the emergence of the "moral self."

LEARNING OBJECTIVES/STUDY QUESTIONS

After reading this chapter, you should be able to:

1. Describe Bronfenbrenner's ecological model for understanding social influences.

2. Identify different types of family structures.

3. Discuss familial factors that influence a child's development.

4. Identify and describe three types of parenting styles identified by Baumrind.

   a.

   b.

   c.

5. Discuss ways in which discipline can enhance or debilitate development.

6. Examine trends observed in the father's role in housework and child care.

7. Summarize the research findings on the effects of working mothers on family life.

8. Examine the different ways in which siblings can affect development.

9. Discuss reasons why the grandparent-grandchild relationship is important.

10. Discuss the different effects on boys and girls of living in single-parent households.

11. Describe some of the common ways in which children react to divorce.

12. Discuss some of the problems faced by stepparents.

13. Discuss trends in foster care and adoption.

14. Identify and describe the four stages in the psychosocial development of friendships.

    a.

    b.

    c.

    d.

15. Describe how peer relationships change from infancy to middle childhood.

16. Describe Robert Selman's five stages in social role taking.

    a. Stage 0 -

    b. Stage 1 -

    c. Stage 2 -

    d. Stage 3 -

    e. Stage 4 -

165

17. Discuss positive and negative effects of television viewing for children.

18. Discuss the effects of computer use among children and concerns about inappropriate materials.

19. Describe the biological, cognitive, and environmental influences on gender roles.

    a. Biological -

    b. Cognitive -

    c. Environmental -

20. Examine how gender-role develops with age.

21. Discuss how younger children's moral reasoning differs from older children's moral reasoning, according to Piaget.

22. Discuss how moral behavior changes over development.

KEY TERMS I

In your own words, provide a definition for each of the following terms:

1. Microsystem_____

_____

2. Mesosystem_____

_____

3. Exosystem_____

_____

4. Macrosystem_____

_____

5. Single-parent family_____

_____

6. Nuclear family_____

_____

7. Extended family_____

_____

8. Blended or reconstituted family_____

_____

9. Stepfamily_____
_____

10. Binuclear family_____
_____

11. Communal family_____
_____

12. Homosexual family_____
_____

13. Cohabitating family_____
_____

14. Generational transmission_____
_____

15. Socialization_____
_____

16. Dysphoria_____
_____

17. Discipline_____
_____

18. Custody_____
_____

19. Legal custody_____
_____

20. Physical custody_____
_____

21. Joint custody_____

22. Visitation rights_____

23. Coparenting_____

24. Parenting coalition_____

25. Open adoption_____

APPLICATIONS I

For each of the following, fill in the blank with one of the terms listed above.

1. Bill's parents constantly argue, and Bill frequently witnesses verbal abuse and physical aggression. As a result, he often blames himself and is afraid of becoming involved in the argument. Their unresolved conflicts leave Bill feeling fear, anger, a sense of helplessness, and _____.

2. When Gina's parents divorced, custody was shared between her mother and father with parental obligations and rights left as they were during the marriage. Gina's parents have joint _____.

3. When there are more than two parenting adults after remarriage, the arrangement is called a _____.

4. Even though Ted's father no longer has custody of him, he does have the right by law to visit Ted every weekend. This is called his _____.

5. Following a divorce, _____ has to do with the issue of where the children will live.

6. In Bronfenbrenner's ecological model, how parental discipline affects the child's behavior in the classroom would be considered part of the _____.

7. The process by which children learn how to fit into their society is called _____.

169

8. Mario, recently divorced, marries Stephanie to form a _____ family.

9. Cultural values and beliefs are considered to be part of the _____ in Bronfenbrenner's model of social influences.

10. Natalie lives with her husband and their six children. This type of family is called a _____.

11. In Bronfenbrenner's ecological model, the child's friends would be included in the _____.

12. Children learn what is expected of them from their parents, who have learned it from their parents. This process of teaching is referred to as _____.

13. Nicole lives part of the time with her mother and stepfather and part of the time with her father. She is part of a _____ family.

14. Susan and Carol, with their two children, live together and are sexually and emotionally committed to one another. They are part of a _____ family.

15. A father is treated badly at work by his boss, and then he takes it out on his children when he gets home. In Bronfenbrenner's model of social influences, what took place at the father's work would be part of the _____.

KEY TERMS II

In your own words, provide a definition for each of the following terms:

1. Autosociality _____

_____

2. Childhood heterosociality _____

_____

3. Homosociality _____

_____

4. Adolescent and adult heterosociality _____

_____

5. Social cognition_____
_____

6. Social role taking_____
_____

7. Egocentric undifferentiated stage_____
_____

8. Differentiated or subjective perspective-taking stage_____
_____

9. Self-reflective thinking or reciprocal perspective-taking stage_____
_____

10. Third-person or mutual perspective-taking stage_____
_____

11. In-depth and societal perspective-taking stage_____
_____

12. Gender_____
_____

13. Gender roles_____
_____

14. Testosterone_____
_____

15. Estrogen_____
_____

16. Gender constancy_____
_____

17. Gender stereotypes_____

_____

18. Androgyny_____

_____

19. Morality of constraint_____

_____

20. Morality of cooperation_____

_____

21. Objective judgments_____

_____

22. Subjective judgments_____

_____

23. Expiatory punishment_____

_____

24. Punishment of reciprocity_____

_____

25. Imminent justice_____

_____

26. Equity_____

_____

APPLICATIONS II

For each of the following, fill in the blank with one of the terms listed above.

1. During infancy and toddlerhood, children prefer to play by themselves or alongside of another child, but not really with another child. This stage is referred to as _____.

2. The period of time in middle childhood during which children prefer to play with others of the same sex is referred to as _____.

3. The capacity to understand social relationships is called _____.

4. When 5-year-old Maggie is asked how her brother feels when she hits him, her response reflects how *she* feels, not how *he* feels. Maggie is in the _____ stage of social role taking.

5. Eight-year-old Stephanie has begun to realize that others have a different point of view and that others are aware that she has a particular point of view. Stephanie is in the _____ stage of social role taking.

6. Our biological sex is referred to as our _____.

7. The feminizing hormone secreted by the ovaries is called _____.

8. Judgments that take into account intention or motives are called _____ judgments.

9. Our outward expressions of masculinity and femininity are referred to as our _____.

10. The idea that only girls like to play with dolls and household items is a _____.

11. A child who can figure out what other people think of her behavior is skilled at _____.

12. A child who understands that she is a girl and will remain a girl, no matter how she dresses or behaves, understands _____.

13. A child who is assertive and independent, yet is also caring and sympathetic towards others may be described as having _____.

14. Children initially believe that rules reflect parental authority and thus, they are inviolable, what Piaget called a morality of _____.

15. According to Piaget, punishment which is imposed by an authority figure is called _____.

SELF-TEST MULTIPLE CHOICE QUESTIONS

Circle the best answer for each question.

1. Bronfenbrenner's ecological model includes all of the following systems, *except*
    a. megasystem.
    b. microsystem.
    c. exosystem.
    d. chronosystem.

2. Due to parental indulgence, Ben has always been the center of attention in his family, and as a result, he has some difficulty in his preschool because he insists on total attention from his peers and teachers. According to Bronfenbrenner, Ben's developmental problems are taking place in the
    a. microsystem.
    b. mesosystem.
    c. exosystem.
    d. macrosystem.

3. What is the term for the family form which consists of a mother, a father, and their children?
    a. nuclear family
    b. blended family
    c. reconstituted family
    d. blended family

4. Diana Baumrind proposed
    a. psychosocial stages.
    b. stages of morality.
    c. styles of play.
    d. parenting styles.

5. Jackie's parents are controlling and adhere rigidly to rules without explaining their reasons. Baumrind classifies Jackie's parents as
    a. indifferent.
    b. authoritarian.
    c. permissive.
    d. authoritative.

6. Leo and Mary use firm control with their children but encourage communication and negotiation in rule setting within the family. What is their parenting style?
    a. authoritative
    b. authoritarian
    c. permissive-indifferent
    d. permissive-indulgent

7. What parenting style has been found to produce the best adjusted children?
   a. permissive
   b. authoritative
   c. indifferent
   d. authoritarian

8. Girls who were raised without their fathers around, in comparison to girls who were raised by both of their parents, were more likely to have
   a. had problems dealing with the opposite sex when they were adolescents.
   b. had sleep disturbances as young children.
   c. had more problems when they were younger than when they were older.
   d. shown masculine behaviors.

9. Children will often begin to play in groups by the time they are
   a. 1 year old.
   b. 18 months.
   c. 2 years.
   d. 3 years.

10. What is the most sophisticated and advanced type of play?
    a. associative
    b. parallel
    c. cooperative
    d. onlooker

11. Megan and Beth agree on the rules for playing hide-and-seek and they spend hours playing this game together. This is an example of what type of play?
    a. onlooker play
    b. cooperative play
    c. unoccupied play
    d. associative play

12. Two preschoolers are sitting at a table side by side, each stacking a different set of blocks. They are engaged in
    a. parallel play.
    b. unoccupied play.
    c. associative play.
    d. cooperative play.

13. Joyce is a disliked child, while Maureen is an unliked child. Which of the following is the best statement regarding these two children?
    a. Joyce is probably very aggressive and obnoxious, while Maureen is more likely shy and withdrawn.
    b. Both Joyce and Maureen will probably be more accepted as they get older.
    c. Maureen is likely to become a disliked child as she gets older, while Joyce is more likely to be accepted later on.
    d. Joyce is likely to remain disliked, while Maureen may very well become accepted as she gets older.

14. Jodie is asked how another child will feel if he is given some milk to drink. She replies that the other child will be unhappy, based on the fact that she herself does not like milk. Jodie reflects which of Selman's developmental stages?
    a. egocentric undifferentiated stage
    b. differentiated or subjective perspective-taking stage
    c. self-reflective thinking or reciprocal perspective-taking stage
    d. third-person or mutual perspective-taking stage

15. Gerald is told a story about how another child had received a gift that she didn't like. Gerald is also shown a picture of this child smiling after having opened the present. When Gerald is asked how he thinks the girl is feeling, he replies "happy," based on how she looks. Gerald is at which of Selman's developmental stages?
    a. egocentric undifferentiated stage
    b. differentiated or subjective perspective-taking stage
    c. self-reflective thinking or reciprocal perspective-taking stage
    d. third-person or mutual perspective-taking stage

16. Research looking at the effects of watching violence on television has found that watching
    a. violence on television causes children to act aggressively.
    b. violence on television is related to increased aggressive behavior.
    c. cartoons lead to more aggressive behavior than watching real people behave violently on television.
    d. violence on television has no effect on children's behavior.

17. Our biological sex, either male or female, is referred to as
    a. gender.
    b. gender roles.
    c. gender constancy.
    d. sex-typing.

18. According to which of the following theories does sex-role identity begin to form when a child realizes that he or she is a boy or girl, and then tries to act consistently with gender expectations?
    a. biological
    b. cognitive
    c. environmental
    d. psychoanalytic

19. A child who thinks that a boy who puts on a dress and plays with dolls will become a girl does not yet understand the concept of
    a. gender constancy.
    b. gender roles.
    c. gender stereotypes.
    d. gender identities.

20. Jack and Molly encourage their three-year-old son to be assertive but at the same time to be warm and tender to help reduce the consequences of viewing the world in terms of gender schemas. They are trying to encourage their son to be
    a. androgynous.
    b. gender-constant.
    c. gender-oriented.
    d. gender-schematic.

21. An androgynous child is one who
    a. has neither masculine nor feminine characteristics.
    b. has both masculine and feminine characteristics.
    c. is either a boy who has only feminine characteristics or is a girl who has only masculine characteristics.
    d. has both male and female biological traits.

22. A child who believes that rules are set by authority figures and cannot be broken believes in a morality of
    a. restriction.
    b. authoritarianism.
    c. cooperation.
    d. constraint.

23. A child who believes in a morality of constraint most likely also believes in the concept of
    a. punishment of reciprocity.
    b. cooperation.
    c. expiatory punishment.
    d. autonomy.

24. Which of the following best describes a morality of constraint?
    a. Rules are unchangeable, and beyond people's control.
    b. Rules and laws are created by people.
    c. Rules are made to be broken.
    d. Each person needs to make up their own rules to live by.

25. A preschooler who expects to be punished immediately after doing something his father told him not to do believes in
    a. internalization.
    b. imminent justice.
    c. autonomous morality.
    d. castration anxiety.

THINKING CRITICALLY ABOUT YOUR DEVELOPMENT

Integrate material from the chapter with your own developmental experiences to respond to the following items.

1. Identify elements of Bronfenbrenner's ecological model that have contributed to your development:

    a. Microsystem -

    b. Mesosystem -

    c. Exosystem -

    d. Macrosystem -

2. What family structure did you grow up in? How did your family transmit knowledge, values, attitudes, roles, and habits?

3. Consider Baumrind's categories of parenting styles: authoritarian, permissive, and authoritative. Which category appears to best represent your own parents' style? Provide examples. Do you exhibit any of the typical developmental consequences of their parenting style?

4. What parental variables influenced your development? How?

5. Did parental discipline enhance or hinder your development? Provide specific examples.

6. Did your parents assign you to help with household chores? What reason did they give for assigning chores? How did you benefit from helping out in the family?

7. Apply what the text says about birth order to your own family. Does it hold true? Why or why not?

8. How did your peer relationship change throughout childhood and adolescence? What psychosocial stages of friendship did you pass through?

9. What were your television viewing habits while growing up? What do you think are the positive and negative effects of television viewing?

10. How has the Internet changed the way that you learn?

ANSWER KEY

APPLICATIONS I

1. dysphoria
2. legal custody
3. parenting coalition
4. visitation rights
5. physical custody
6. mesosystem
7. socialization
8. blended or reconstituted
9. macrosystem
10. nuclear family
11. microsystem
12. generational transmission
13. binuclear
14. homosexual
15. exosystem

APPLICATIONS II

1. autosociality
2. homosociality
3. social cognition
4. egocentric undifferentiated
5. self-reflective thinking or reciprocal perspective-taking
6. gender
7. estrogen
8. subjective
9. gender roles
10. gender stereotype
11. social role-taking
12. gender constancy
13. androgyny
14. constraint
15. expiatory punishment

MULTIPLE CHOICE

1. a	6. a	11. b	16. b	21. b
2. b	7. b	12. a	17. a	22. d
3. a	8. a	13. a	18. b	23. c
4. d	9. d	14. a	19. a	24. a
5. b	10. c	15. b	20. a	25. b

Chapter 10
PERSPECTIVES ON ADOLESCENT DEVELOPMENT

CHAPTER OUTLINE & OVERVIEW

I. The meaning of adolescence

    A. Adolescence - Adolescence is a period of growth beginning with puberty and ending at the beginning of adulthood.

    B. Puberty and pubescence
        1. Puberty is the period at which a person reaches sexual maturity and becomes capable of having children.
        2. Pubescence describes the period during which physical changes relative to sexual maturation are taking place. Psychological and social changes take place as well.

    C. Maturity - Maturity is the age, state, or time of life at which a person is considered fully developed socially, intellectually, emotionally, physically, and spiritually.

    D. Juvenile - The word juvenile is a legal term describing an individual who is not accorded adult status in the eyes of the law. In most states, this is a person under 18 years of age.

    E. Transition to adulthood – The transition to adulthood evidently takes place not in the form of discrete transition events but according to the individual's judgment of when various subtle psychological processes have been reached.

II. Adolescence and psychic disequilibrium

    A. Storm and stress
        1. G. Stanley Hall described adolescence as a period of great storm and stress, the causes of which are biological.
        2. Researchers no longer believe that storm and stress are inevitable consequences of adolescence.

    B. Psychic conflict
        1. Anna Freud characterized adolescence as a period of psychic disequilibrium, emotional conflict, and erratic behavior.
        2. Instinctual forces that have remained latent since early childhood reappear.
        3. The increasing demands of the id during adolescence create conflict with the superego, which the ego must try to resolve. If this id-ego-superego conflict is not resolved during adolescence, emotional disturbance results.

4. Harmony among the id, ego, and superego is possible and does occur finally in most normal adolescents.

III. Adolescence and identity achievement

    A. Components of identity
1. Identity has many components - sexual, social, physical, psychological, moral, ideological, and vocational.
2. Some components of identity are established before others.
3. Gender differences are sometimes evident in the identity development process.

    B. Psychosocial moratorium - Erikson described a period of adolescence during which the individual may stand back, analyze, and experiment with various roles without assuming any one role.

    C. Identity statuses
1. Marcia formulated four identity statuses: identity achievement, moratorium, foreclosure, and identity diffusion. These do not always develop in exact sequence.
2. Three important variations from this developmental sequence have been observed.
    a. Some individuals seem never to make the transition to the moratorium and identity statuses, remaining entrenched within the foreclosure status.
    b. A significant number of individuals enter adolescence in the diffusion status; some of these remain diffused.
    c. Certain individuals who attain an achievement status appear to have regressed to a lower status on follow-up years later.

    D. Ethnic identity
1. Ethnic identity is the sum total of group members' feelings about those values, symbols, and common histories that identify them as a distinct group.
2. In high school and college students, ethnic identity appears to consist of a single factor, including three intercorrelated components: positive ethnic attitudes, ethnic identity achievement, and ethnic behaviors. Acculturation is the adjustment of minority groups to the culture of the dominant group.
3. The problem for adolescents from immigrant or ethnic minority families is that the culture into which they were born is not always valued or appreciated by the culture in which they are raised.
4. There are four possible ways in which ethnic group members can participate in a culturally diverse society: assimilation, integration, separation, and marginality. Of the four acculturation options, integration results in better psychological adjustment and higher self-esteem.
5. Gifted black students may experience more psychological and emotional problems than do black students not identified as gifted.

6. Research on ethnic identity exploration and commitment among Native American adolescents reveals that school context has a marked effect on ethnic identity commitment.

IV. Adolescence and developmental tasks

   A. Meaning - Developmental tasks are the knowledge, attitudes, functions, and skills that individuals must acquire at certain points in their lives through physical maturation, personal effort, and social expectations.

   B. Havighurst's eight major tasks:
      1. Accepting one's physique and using the body effectively
      2. Achieving emotional independence from parents and other adults
      3. Achieving a masculine or feminine social-sex role
      4. Achieving new and more mature relations with age-mates of both sexes
      5. Desiring and achieving socially responsible behavior
      6. Acquiring a set of values and an ethical system as a guide to behavior
      7. Preparing for an economic career
      8. Preparing for marriage and family life

V. Anthropologists' views of adolescence

   A. Developmental continuity versus discontinuity - Anthropologists, such as Margaret Mead, emphasize continuity of development rather than the discontinuity of different stages.

   B. Cultural influences - Anthropologists say that storm and stress during adolescence is not inevitable.

   C. Generation gap - Although anthropologists deny the inevitability of a generation gap, they describe the many conditions in Western culture that create such a gap, such as pluralistic value systems, rapid social change, modern technology, early physiological puberty, and the prolongation of adolescence.

VI. Critique - One perspective of adolescence gives only a partial picture; one must take into account many points of view to develop the fullest understanding of adolescence.

LEARNING OBJECTIVES/STUDY QUESTIONS

After reading this chapter, you should be able to:

1. Discuss why G. Stanley Hall believes that adolescence is a time of "storm and stress."

2. Discuss Anna Freud's concept of psychic conflict in adolescence and how it can become problematic.

3. Describe the components of identity.

4. Define psychosocial moratorium.

5. Identify and describe Marcia's four identity statuses.

6. Define ethnic identity.

7. Identify and describe four possible ways in which ethnic group members can participate in a culturally diverse society.

8. List Havighurst's eight major psychosocial tasks to be accomplished during adolescence.

   a.

   b.

   c.

   d.

   e.

   f.

   g.

   h.

9. Discuss anthropologists' views of adolescence.

KEY TERMS

In your own words, provide a definition for each of the following terms:

1. Puberty _____

_____

2. Pubescence _____

_____

3. Maturity _____

_____

4. Juvenile _____

_____

5. Psychosocial moratorium _____

_____

6. Identity achievement _____

_____

7. Moratorium _____

_____

8. Foreclosure _____

_____

9. Identity diffusion _____

_____

10. Acculturation _____

_____

11. Developmental tasks _____

_____

APPLICATIONS

For each of the following, fill in the blank with one of the terms listed above.

1. Angela, an African-American adolescent, has difficulty adjusting to the white culture. This adjustment is called __acculturation__

2. Bill has grown as much as he ever will; he can be said to have reached physical __maturity__

3. Tom has not experienced an identity crisis nor explored meaningful alternatives in trying to find an identity. Tom has adopted the identity status of __id diffusion__

4. Sandra is an early maturer who finds that along with changes in her physical appearance, she experiences changes in social interests and friendships. This period of change is called __pubescence__.

5. Achieving emotional independence from parents and other adults is a __developmental task__ outlined by Havighurst.

6. A 14-year-old who commits a crime would be treated in the eyes of the law as a __juvenile__ rather than as an adult.

7. The period of time between childhood and adulthood where an individual can spend some time exploring different roles without feeling pressured to know just what he or she wants is referred to as __moratorium__

8. Donna has started menstruating and she is now capable of reproduction. She has reached __puberty__.

9. Ron's parents are both lawyers. Since he was a young boy, his parents told him that he too should become a lawyer. When Ron's tenth-grade teacher asked him to write an essay on what he wanted to do with his life, Ron wrote about how he would become a lawyer. Ron has adopted the identity status of __foreclosure__.

10. For several years, Dana agonized over whether she should go to business school or a liberal arts school. After thinking it through very carefully, she decided to go to business school, and she was proud of her decision. Dana has adopted the identity status of __id achievement__

SELF-TEST MULTIPLE CHOICE QUESTIONS

Circle the best answer for each question.

1. The developmental stage that lies between childhood and adulthood is called
    - (a.) puberty.
    - b. young adulthood.
    - c. latency.
    - d. adolescence.

2. The period at which a person reaches sexual maturity and becomes capable of reproduction is called
    - (a.) puberty.
    - b. maturity.
    - c. pubescence.
    - d. adolescence.

3. The age, state, or time of life at which a person is considered fully developed socially, intellectually, emotionally, physically, and spiritually defines
    - (a.) maturity.
    - b. puberty.
    - c. pubescence.
    - d. adulthood.

4. The period during which physical changes relative to sexual maturation take place is called
    - a. the maturational stage.
    - b. the stage of sexual transformation.
    - c. adolescent turmoil.
    - (d.) pubescence.

5. Who characterized adolescence from a psychoanalytical point of view as a period of psychic disequilibrium, emotional conflict, and erratic behavior?
    - a. G. Stanley Hall
    - (b.) Anna Freud
    - c. Margaret Mead
    - d. Robert Havighurst

6. The time in life when one becomes an adult physically, emotionally, socially, intellectually, and spiritually defines
    - a. puberty.
    - (b.) maturity.
    - c. pubescence.
    - d. adolescence.

7. Who described the defense mechanisms of asceticism and intellectualism that appears during adolescence?
   a. James Marcia
   b. Anna Freud
   c. Erik Erikson
   d. G. Stanley Hall

8. According to Erikson, the major psychosocial task of adolescence is the achievement of
   a. autonomy.
   b. industry.
   c. identity.
   d. generativity.

9. Which component of identity is likely to develop first?
   a. physical
   b. vocational
   c. moral
   d. ideological

10. James Marcia is associated with
    a. achievement motivation.
    b. developmental tasks.
    c. parenting styles.
    d. identity statuses.

11. Veronica has gone through a crisis, and as a result, now pursues personally chosen goals. Veronica has reached the status of
    a. moratorium.
    b. diffusion.
    c. achievement.
    d. foreclosure.

12. Before Jeff had had the opportunity to explore his vocation on his own, his parents told him that he was expected to take over the family restaurant after graduating, and Jeff readily agreed. Which identity status has Jeff adopted?
    a. diffusion
    b. foreclosure
    c. moratorium
    d. achievement

13. Research shows that personality type is related to identity status. In one study (Clancy & Dollinger, 1993), which subjects scored higher than the typical student on extraversion and lower on neuroticism?
    a. foreclosed subjects
    b. diffused subjects
    c. identity-achieved subjects
    d. moratorium subjects

14. As 18-year-old Jack seeks to find out what distinguishes him from others, he decides to take time off and travel abroad for a year before attending college. Jack is pursuing
    a. identity diffusion.
    b. a psychological moratorium.
    c. identity foreclosure.
    d. identity achievement.

15. What term did Erikson use to describe a period of adolescence during which the individual may stand back, analyze, and experiment with various roles without assuming any one role?
    a. psychosocial diffusion
    b. psychosocial moratorium
    c. psychosocial achievement
    d. psychosocial foreclosure

16. Which of the following identity statuses is the *most* developmentally advanced?
    a. identity achievement
    b. moratorium
    c. foreclosure
    d. identity diffusion

17. Rajeesh moved to the United States from Pakistan several years ago with his family. He has adjusted well to his new school and has many new friends, many of whom are white. He also believes that it is important to know as much as possible about his own ethnic background. He is proud of his history, and follows the customs very closely. Which acculturation option has Rajeesh chosen?
    a. assimilation
    b. marginality
    c. separation
    d. integration

18. A child who is rebellious against her parents may be trying to resolve which developmental task as suggested by Havighurst?
    a. accepting one's physique and using the body effectively
    b. achieving emotional independence from parents and other adults
    c. desiring and achieving socially responsible behavior
    d. acquiring a set of values and an ethical system as a guide to behavior

19. An adolescent who has recently become very involved in working with conservation groups in her community may be working on which of Havighurst's developmental tasks?
    a. achieving a masculine or feminine social-sex role
    b. desiring and achieving socially responsible behavior
    c. acquiring a set of values and an ethical system as a guide to behavior
    d. preparing for an economic career

20. Who outlined eight major psychosocial developmental tasks to be accomplished during adolescence?
    a. James Marcia
    b. G. Stanley Hall
    c. Erik Erikson
    d. Robert Havighurst ✓

21. "Achieving a masculine or feminine social-sex role" is an example of a(n)
    a. defense mechanism.
    b. identity status.
    c. psychosocial moratorium.
    d. developmental task. ✓

22. Chan is from China. Now studying at a midwestern university, he decides to have nothing to do with the larger, dominant white culture. He focuses exclusively on the cultural values and practices of his Chinese culture. Chan's behavior illustrates
    a. assimilation.
    b. integration.
    c. marginality.
    d. separation. ✓

23. The absence or loss of one's culture of origin and the lack of involvement with the dominant society defines
    a. assimilation.
    b. integration.
    c. marginality.
    d. separation. ✓

24. Since Bev immigrated from Bosnia, she has lost contact with her traditional culture and does not become involved in American society. This illustrates
    a. assimilation.
    b. integration.
    c. marginality. ✓
    d. separation.

25. Whom of the following emphasized continuity of development for adolescents?
    a. Anna Freud
    b. Margaret Mead ✓
    c. Robert Havighurst
    d. G. Stanley Hall

CRITICALLY THINKING ABOUT YOUR DEVELOPMENT

Integrate material from the chapter with your own developmental experiences to respond to the following items.

1. Was G. Stanley Hall correct in describing adolescence as a period of great "storm and stress?" For you, was adolesence a time of "storm and stress?" What does that phrase mean to you?

2. What rites of passage have you experienced?

3. Which identity status have you adopted?

4. Did you experience what Anna Freud thought of as a psychic conflict during adolescence? In what way?

5. How many of Havinghurst's eight major tasks of adolesence have you accomplished? Which ones? Are the others worth accomplishing? If so, what has prevented you from accomplishing them?

ANSWER KEY

APPLICATIONS

1. acculturation
2. maturity
3. identity diffusion
4. pubescence
5. developmental task
6. juvenile
7. psychosocial moratorium
8. puberty
9. foreclosure
10. identity achievement

MULTIPLE CHOICE

1.	d	6.	b	11.	d	16.	a	21.	d
2.	a	7.	b	12.	b	17.	d	22.	d
3.	a	8.	c	13.	c	18.	b	23.	d
4.	d	9.	a	14.	b	19.	b	24.	c
5.	b	10.	d	15.	b	20.	d	25.	b

Chapter 11
PHYSICAL DEVELOPMENT

CHAPTER OUTLINE & OVERVIEW

I. The endocrine glands and hypothalamus – The endocrine gland is a gland that secretes hormones internally.

    A. Pituitary gland - The pituitary gland is located in the base of the brain and produces hormones that regulate growth.

    B. Gonads - The gonads, or sex glands, include the ovaries in the female and the testes in the male.

    C. Adrenals and hypothalamus
        1. The adrenal glands are located just above the kidneys.
        2. The hypothalamus is a small area of the forebrain that regulates such functions as lactation, pregnancy, menstrual cycles, hormonal production, drinking, eating, and sexual response and behavior.

II. Maturation and functions of sex organs

    A. Male
        1. The primary male sex organs are the penis, scrotum, testes, prostate gland, seminal vesicles, epididymis, Cowper's glands, urethra, and vas deferens.
        2. Important changes occur in the male sex organs during adolescence, the most important of which is the development of mature sperm cells.
        3. Adolescent boys may become concerned about nocturnal emissions. Anxiety may be prevented if adolescents are prepared for them before they occur.

    B. Female
        1. The primary internal female sex organs are the vagina, fallopian tubes, uterus, and ovaries. The external female sex organs are known collectively as the vulva.
        2. Many changes occur in the female internal and external sex organs during adolescence.

    C. Menstruation
        1. The average age of menarche is 12 to 13 years, although this varies considerably.
        2. The time of ovulation is ordinarily about 14 days before the onset of the next menstrual period.

    D. Factors in timing - Heredity and ethnic factors, nutrition, medical care, diet and exercise, and stress can all affect the timing of sexual maturation.

III. Physical growth and development

   A. Development of secondary sexual characteristics
      1. Sexual maturation at puberty also includes the development of secondary sexual characteristics, such as the development of mature female and male body contours, voice changes, the appearance of body hair, and other minor changes.
      2. The average girl matures about 2 years before the average boy, but the time of development is not always consistent.

   B. Growth in height and weight
      1. A growth spurt in height begins in early adolescence and is accompanied by an increase in weight and changes in body proportions.
      2. One of the most important factors in determining the total mature height of the individual is heredity.
      3. The growth achieved before puberty is of greater significance to total adult height than is the growth achieved during puberty.

IV. Early and late maturation

   A. Early-maturing boys - Early-maturing boys have both athletic and social advantages.

   B. Early-maturing girls - Girls who mature early are at a disadvantage during the elementary school years, but may be at an advantage during junior high and high school age.

   C. Late-maturing boys - Late-maturing boys suffer a number of social disadvantages and may develop feelings of inferiority as a result.

   D. Late-maturing girls - Late-maturing girls of junior or senior high school age are often socially handicapped.

V. Body image and psychological impact

   A. Physical attractiveness
      1. Attractiveness affects the adolescent's positive self-esteem and social acceptance. Also, it affects personality, interpersonal attraction, and social relationships.
      2. There is a definite link between body esteem and self-esteem.

   B. Concepts of the Ideal
      1. Adolescents' self-appraisals of their physical attractiveness are determined partly by comparing themselves with other persons around them.
      2. It is partly because of our obsession with slimness that anorexia nervosa and bulimia develop among adolescents.

VI. Sex education of adolescents

   A. Goals - Some of the goals of sex education include: gaining knowledge about bodily changes and basic facts about human reproduction, developing sexual health, preventing unwanted pregnancies and sexually transmitted diseases.

   B. The parents' role - Some parents do not do a good job discussing sex education with their children. Some may be uncomfortable or uninformed. Others may want to avoid experimentation.

   C. The school's role
       1. Nationwide surveys indicate that about 85 percent of parents favor sex education in the schools.
       2. Many schools are taking the responsibility for teaching sex education in an attempt to reach as many children as possible.
       3. The major problem teachers face in providing sex education is negative pressure from parents, the community, or the school administration. Teachers need to be provided with training, support, and agreed-on guidelines on methodology and procedures.

VII. Nutrition and weight

   A. Caloric requirements - During the period of rapid growth, adolescents need greater quantities of food to take care of bodily requirements.

   B. Importance of nutrition - Health maintenance depends partly on proper eating habits.

   C. Deficiencies - Many adolescents have diets that are deficient in thiamine and riboflavin, other vitamins, calcium, iron, and/or protein.

   D. Overweight and underweight - Being overweight or underweight affects the adolescent's emotional adjustment, self-esteem, and social relationships.

   E. Anorexia nervosa - Anorexia nervosa is a life-threatening emotional disorder characterized by an obsession with being slender.

   F. Bulimia - Bulimia is a binge-purge syndrome.

LEARNING OBJECTIVES/STUDY QUESTIONS

After reading this chapter, you should be able to:

1. Discuss the functions of the pituitary gland, the adrenal glands, the gonads, and the hypothalamus.

    a. Pituitary gland -

    b. Adrenal glands -

    c. Gonads -

    d. Hypothalamus -

2. Discuss the maturation and functions of the male and female sex organs.

    a. Male -

    b. Female -

3. Discuss factors that affect the timing of sexual maturation.

4. Discuss the development of the secondary sexual characteristics.

5. Discuss factors which affect growth in height and weight.

6. Describe the psychological effects of early and late maturation for boys and girls.

    a. Early-maturing boys -

    b. Early-maturing girls -

    c. Late-maturing boys -

    d. Late-maturing girls -

7. Discuss the impact of physical attractiveness on adolescents' psychological development.

8. What are the goals of sex education? What role do parents and the schools play?

9. Explain the importance of good nutrition in adolescence.

10. Distinguish between anorexia nervosa and bulimia.

KEY TERMS I

In your own words, provide a definition for each of the following terms:

1. Endocrine gland _____
   _____

2. Hormones _____
   _____

3. Pituitary gland _____
   _____

4. Gonadotropic hormones _____
   _____

5. Follicle-stimulating hormone _____
   _____

6. Luteinizing hormone _____
   _____

7. Human growth hormone _____
   _____

8. Prolactin _____
   _____

9. Gonads _____

_____

10. Estrogens _____

_____

11. Progesterone _____

_____

12. Corpus lutem _____

_____

13. Adrenal glands _____

_____

14. Hypothalamus _____

_____

15. Gonadotropin-releasing hormone (GnRH) _____

_____

16. Penis _____

_____

17. Scrotum _____

_____

18. Testes _____

_____

19. Prostate gland _____

_____

20. Seminal vesicles _____

_____

21. Epididymis_____

APPLICATIONS I

For each of the following, fill in the blank with one of the terms listed above.

1. The sex glands are referred to as the __gonads__.

2. The egg cell is called the __ovum__.

3. The __adrenals__ are located just above the kidneys; they secrete adrenalin as well as androgens and estrogens in both men and women.

4. The __LH__ hormone stimulates development of the ovum, as well as estrogen and progesterone in females, and sperm and testosterone in males.

5. A group of female hormones called __estrogens__ are produced by the ovaries, and to some extent by the adrenal glands, in both males and females.

6. The biochemical substances that are secreted into the bloodstream by the endocrine glands are called __hormones__.

7. The secretion of milk by a nursing mother is stimulated by __prolactin__.

8. The __hypothalamus__ is the small area of the brain controlling motivation, emotion, pleasure, and pain in the body.

9. The master gland of the body that produces hormones that regulate growth is the __pituitary gland__

10. The female sex hormone produced by the corpus luteum of the ovary is called __progesterone__

11. The pituitary hormone that regulates overall body growth is __HGH__.

12. The hormone that controls the production and release of FSH and LH from the pituitary is the __gonadotropin releasing__ hormone.

13. Ductless glands that secrete hormones are called __endocrine__ glands.

14. The external female sex organs are known collectively as the __vulva__.

15. The __prostate__ gland secretes a portion of the seminal fluid.

KEY TERMS II

In your own words, provide a definition for each of the following terms:

1. Cowper's glands _____

2. Urethra _____

3. Vas deferens _____

4. Nocturnal emissions _____

5. Vagina _____

6. Fallopian tubes _____

7. Uterus _____

8. Ovaries _____

9. Vulva _____

10. Hymen _____

11. Bartholin's glands _____

12. Labia majora_____

13. Labia minora_____

14. Clitoris_____

15. Mons veneris_____

16. Menarche_____

17. Secondary sexual characteristics_____

18. Primary sexual characteristics_____

19. Anorexia nervosa_____

20. Bulimia_____

APPLICATIONS II

For each of the following, fill in the blank with one of the terms listed above.

1. In some instances, conception can occur even if the male has withdrawn his penis prior to ejaculation because the alkaline fluid secreted by the __Cowper's gland__ sometimes contains sperm.

2. An adolescent boy who has an erotic dream that culminates in an orgasm has experienced what is referred to as a __nocturnal emission__

205

3. The primary internal female sex organs are the __vagina__, fallopian tubes, uterus, and ovaries.

4. The mons pubis, also known as the __mons veneris__, becomes more prominent through the development of a fatty pad.

5. An eating disorder characterized by bingeing and purging is called __bulimia__.

6. The large outer lips of tissue on either side of the vaginal opening are the __labia majora__

7. The womb in which the baby grows and develops is the __uterus__.

8. In females, __menarche__ usually does not occur until maximum growth rates in height and weight have been achieved.

9. The tissue that partly covers the vaginal opening is called the __hymen__.

10. An adolescent who is obsessed with being thin, and has lost an excessive amount of weight for her body size may have __anorexia nervosa__

11. The adolescent boy's changing voice and growth of facial and pubic hair are considered to be __secondary sexual charact.__

12. The glands on either side of the vaginal opening that secrete fluid during sexual excitement are the __Bartholin's glands__

13. The tubes that transport the ova from the ovaries to the uterus are the __fallopian tubes__

14. The external female sex organs are known collectively as the __vulva__.

15. Changes that involve the sex organs at sexual maturation are called __primary sexual charact.__

SELF-TEST MULTIPLE CHOICE QUESTIONS

Circle the best answer for each question.

1. What gland is referred to as the master gland and produces hormones that regulate growth?
    a. adrenal gland
    b. Cowper's gland
    c. prostate gland
    d. pituitary gland

2. What hormone affects the overall growth and shaping of the skeleton?
    a. gonadotropic hormone
    b. luteinizing hormone
    c. follicle-stimulating hormone
    d. human growth hormone

3. Which of the following hormones affects the secretion of milk by the mammary glands of the breast?
    a. follicle-stimulating hormone
    b. luteinizing hormone
    c. prolactin
    d. human growth hormone

4. The development of male or female characteristics is partly determined by the
    a. presence or absence of male versus female hormones.
    b. ratio of the levels of male to female hormones.
    c. presence or absence of estrogens.
    d. presence or absence of androgens.

5. What hormone controls the secretion of FSH and LH from the pituitary?
    a. gonadotropin-releasing hormone
    b. luteinizing hormone
    c. follicle-stimulating hormone
    d. human growth hormone

6. What is the motivational and emotional control center of the brain?
    a. adrenal gland
    b. pituitary gland
    c. hypothalamus
    d. prostate gland

7. Which of the following is *not* a primary male sex organ?
    a. uterus
    b. urethra
    c. prostate gland
    d. vas deferens

8. The follicles usually produce a mature ovum about once
    a. every two hours.
    b. every 14 days.
    c. every 28 days.
    d. a year.

9. First menstruation is called
    a. menses.
    b. dysmenorrhea.
    c. menarche.
    d. menopause.

10. Which of the following is responsible for sexual maturation in males?
    a. estrogen
    b. testosterone
    c. progesterone
    d. androgen

11. The time of ovulation is usually
    a. about 14 days before the onset of the next menstrual period.
    b. about 14 days after the onset of the menstrual period.
    c. during the menstrual period.
    d. about 7 days after the onset of the menstrual period.

12. Jeff has noticed that his voice is beginning to change, the shape of his body is changing, and he is growing pubic and facial hair. What he is noticing is the development of
    a. primary sexual characteristics.
    b. secondary sexual characteristics.
    c. deciduous sexual characteristics.
    d. latent sexual characteristics.

13. The average girl matures about
    a. the same time as the average boy.
    b. 1 year before the average boy.
    c. 2 years before the average boy.
    d. 2 years after the average boy.

14. The adolescent girls begins menstruating at an average age of
    a. 9 to 11 years.
    b. 12 to 13 years.
    c. 13 to 15 years.
    d. 15 to 16 years.

15. Which of the following is *not* a primary sexual characteristic?
    a. menstruation
    b. vaginal changes
    c. growth of the penis and scrotum
    d. development of breasts

16. Which of the following is a primary sexual characteristic in males?
    a. height spurt
    b. growth of penis
    c. marked voice change
    d. growth of beard

17. Which of the following is a primary sexual characteristic in females?
    a. menarche
    b. deepening of voice
    c. height spurt
    d. curly pubic hair

18. Early-maturing girls
    a. are more likely to be at a social advantage than early maturing boys when they are in elementary school.
    b. are likely to start dating later than most.
    c. are at a disadvantage in elementary school, but in junior high and high school, may be at a social advantage.
    d. are less likely than late-maturing girls to have parents that worry about them and try to restrain their activities.

19. Which of the following statements about early-maturing boys is true?
    a. They are more popular than late-maturing boys.
    b. They have a more difficult adjustment than late-maturing boys.
    c. They are overly concerned with matters related to social acceptance.
    d. They tend to have higher IQs.

20. What percent of parents favor sex education in the schools?
    a. 10 percent
    b. 33 percent
    c. 50 percent
    d. 85 percent

21. What percent of all adolescents are obese?
    a. 3 to 5 percent
    b. 10 to 15 percent
    c. 22 to 25 percent
    d. 30 to 35 percent

22. Fearing womanhood, Eileen stops eating, thereby halting her body's development. She is obsessed by thoughts of food and an unattainable image of "perfect" thinness. What is her disorder?
    a. pica
    b. binge-eating
    c. bulimia
    d. anorexia nervosa

23. Lauren's therapist believes that her anorexia nervosa is caused by a power struggle between Lauren and her mother. Lauren's therapist adheres to what theory?
    a. social theory
    b. psychosexual theory
    c. family systems theory
    d. psychobiologic regression hypothesis

209

24. Monica is terribly anxious about weighing too much but has an uncontrollable need to eat, especially sweets. She consumes huge quantities of food in an hour, and then feels despondent and out of control. To compensate for overeating, she vomits. What is her disorder?
    a. pica
    b. bulimia
    c. anorexia nervosa
    d. binge-eating

25. What theory of the cause of anorexia nervosa suggests that it is caused by a sexual conflict in which the individual is unwilling to accept adult sexuality, fears sexual intimacy, and thus tries to delay sexual development?
    a. psychobiological repression theory
    b. psychosexual theory
    c. family systems theory
    d. social theory

THINKING CRITICALLY ABOUT YOUR DEVELOPMENT

Integrate material from the chapter with your own developmental experiences to respond to the following items.

1. What psychological affect did your sexual maturation have on you?

2. Were you an early-maturer or late-maturer in your development? If so, how did that affect your psychological and social adjustment? Did your experience support the research on maturation effects?

3. What role did your physical attractiveness play in your adolescent psychological development?

4. What social pressures influenced your perceptions of body image and appearance in adolescence, if any?

5. What role did your parents play in discussing sex education with you?

ANSWER KEY

APPLICATIONS I

1. gonads
2. ovum
3. adrenal glands
4. luteinizing
5. estrogens
6. hormones
7. prolactin
8. hypothalamus
9. pituitary gland
10. progesterone
11. human growth hormone
12. gonadotropin-releasing
13. endocrine
14. vulva
15. prostate

APPLICATIONS II

1. Cowper's gland
2. nocturnal emission
3. vagina
4. mons veneris
5. bulimia
6. labia majora
7. uterus
8. menarche
9. hymen
10. anorexia nervosa
11. secondary sexual characteristics
12. Bartholin's glands
13. fallopian tubes
14. vulva
15. primary sexual characteristics

MULTIPLE CHOICE

1. d
2. d
3. c
4. b
5. a
6. c
7. a
8. c
9. c
10. b
11. a
12. b
13. c
14. b
15. d
16. b
17. a
18. c
19. a
20. d
21. b
22. d
23. c
24. b
25. b

Chapter 12
COGNITIVE DEVELOPMENT

CHAPTER OUTLINE & OVERVIEW

I. Formal operational thought

    A. Characteristics
1. In formal operations, one can reason, systematize ideas, construct theories, and test them.
2. Adolescent thought can maneuver between reality and possibility.
3. Formal operational adolescents are flexible.
4. Formal operational adolescents can use a set of symbols.
5. Adolescents can orient themselves toward what is abstract and not immediately present.
6. Formal operational thinking involves introspection, abstract thinking, logical thinking, and hypothetical reasoning.

    B. Effects on personality and behavior
1. Idealism - The ability to distinguish the possible from the real allows them to imagine ideal circumstances and to focus on long-term implications.
2. Discrepancy - Early adolescents can formulate general principles but they have difficulty with specific practices.
3. Self-consciousness and egocentrism - The capacity to think about their own thoughts makes adolescents become acutely aware of themselves.
4. Conformity - Adolescents have a greater potential for creativity but in reality they are less creative because of pressures to conform.
5. Decentering and a life plan - True integration into society comes when the adolescent begins to affirm a life plan and adopt a social role.

    C. Achieving formal operational thought
1. Ages and percentages - There is a great deal of variability in the age at which formal operations is achieved, and some individuals may never achieve it.
2. Test level - The percentages of people reaching formal operations is dependent on the measures used to evaluate it.
3. Maturation and intelligence - Maturation of the nervous system plays an important role in cognitive development, because the nervous system must be sufficiently developed for any real thought to take place. It is the interaction of age and intelligence that contributes to cognitive ability.
4. Cross-cultural studies - Formal thought is more dependent on social experience than is sensorimotor or concrete operational thought.

D. Adolescent education and formal operational thought - According to Piaget, the two goals of education are to create individuals who are capable of doing new things, and to form minds which can be critical.

E. Problem-finding stage - There may be a fifth stage of development, called a problem-finding stage, which is characterized by the ability to create, to discover, and to formulate problems.

II. Scholastic aptitude

    A. Scholastic Aptitude Test (SAT)
        1. The SAT was one of the most widely used tests in the United States. It is supposed to measure basic abilities; however, some research has indicated that coaching and cramming could improve scores.
        2. The total SAT scores of college-bound seniors declined until 1980, then showed some increase.

    B. Revisions of the SAT
        1. The College Board approved changes in the SAT in 1995. The test is now known as the Scholastic Assessment Test.
        2. Proponents claim it is less coachable than the old test.

    C. ACT
        1. Some authorities suggest that achievement tests would be a better way of predicting college success than SATs.
        2. The ACT Assessment Program is the second most widely used college admissions test. The academic tests include tests in math, English, reading, and science reasoning.

III. School

    A. Trends in American education
        1. Progressives versus traditionalists
            a. Progressives have argued that the goal of education is to prepare students for all phases of life.
            b. Traditionalists have argued that the goal of education is to teach the basics.
        2. Goals of progressive education – The schoolroom should be a laboratory of living, preparing students for all of life. As a consequence, many schools introduced vocational and personal service courses.
        3. After Sputnik – The National Defense Education Act appropriated $1 billion in federal aid to education, which supported the teaching of science, math, and foreign languages.

4. 1960s and 1970s – The schools were called on to rescue a society that was in turmoil. Major school aid legislation was passed as part of the Johnson administration's "War on Poverty." Career and experimental education replaced academic programs so that adolescents could receive "hands-on" experience.
5. 1980s and 1990s – By 1980, people became alarmed at the decline in academic indicators. The pendulum began to swing back to a more traditionalist position.

B. Middle schools and junior high schools
1. One of the problems of modern schools stems partly from their size. Ideally, the best schools seek to combine academic excellence with personalized attention and services to achieve both intellectual rigor and intimacy.
2. One of the answers has been the formation of schools in which older students are taken out of the upper elementary grades and put in middle schools, and eighth and ninth grade students are taken out of high schools and put in junior high schools.

C. Enrollment in high school - In 1950, only 33 percent of those 25 and over had completed four or more years of high school. By 1997, the number was 82.1 percent.

D. Types of high schools - Families that can afford private education are more likely to get superior education for their adolescents than if they sent them to the average public school.

E. Cultural differences in achievement
1. There are cross-national differences in academic achievement. Students in East Asian countries consistently outperform their American peers, especially in mathematics and science.
2. Time at school – The Japanese and Chinese students were at school each school day an hour or two longer than the American students.
3. Work and major activities
   a. While 80 percent of the American teenagers held part-time jobs, only 26 percent of the Chinese students and 27 percent of the Japanese students worked at jobs outside of school.
   b. American students spent about 80 percent more time with their friends than they did studying. Chinese students spent nearly twice as much time studying as they did with their friends.
4. Extracurricular activities – Schooling and adacemic activities appeared to be more important to East Asian adolescents, while peers and the workplace tended to be relatively more important to most American teenagers.

F. Cross-cultural achievement and psychological adjustment - High academic achievement, such as that exhibited by students in Taiwan and Japan, can be obtained without necessarily increasing students' reports of psychological distress.

G. Dropouts
1. Most dropouts occur during the high school years, especially after age 17.
2. There are numerous reasons for dropping out of school, including: family relationships, pregnancy and marriage, money and employment, social adjustment and peer associations, school apathy, truancy, personality, stress, socioeconomic factors, and ethnic identity.
3. Intervention programs can reduce the dropout rate considerably.

H. Academic success
1. Schools need to be kept small and their adult populations accessible.
2. Schools need to create an atmosphere that promotes positive peer relationships and helps students develop social skills.
3. Schools need to provide youth with an authentic experience of personal success.

I. Full-service schools - Full-service schools integrate education, medical, social, and/or human services that are beneficial to children and youth and their families on school grounds or at other locations that are easily accessible. Full-service schools provide the types of prevention, treatment, and support services that children and families need to succeed.

LEARNING OBJECTIVES/STUDY QUESTIONS

After reading this chapter, you should be able to:

1. Describe the characteristics of Piaget's formal operational stage.

2. Describe some of the effects of formal operational thought on adolescents' personality and behavior.

3. Examine how the development of formal operations problem solving can be encouraged in the school.

4. Describe the problem-finding stage.

5. Compare the use of the SAT and the ACT in predicting college success.

6. Describe trends in the American education system over the past 50 years in terms of the use of a progressive or a traditionalist approach.

7. Explain how middle schools and junior high schools help in the transition from elementary school to high school.

8. Compare four types of high schools: public, Catholic, elite private boarding schools, and elite high performance private schools.

9. Examine cultural differences in achievement.

10. Identify factors associated with dropping out of high school.

11. Identify factors that are important in enabling students to achieve academically.

12. Describe full-service schools.

KEY TERMS

In your own words, provide a definition for each of the following terms:

1. Sociocentrism_____

_____

2. Personal fable_____

_____

3. Problem-finding stage_____

_____

4. Scholastic Aptitude Test (SAT)_____

_____

5. ACT Assessment Program (American College Testing Program)_____

_____

6. Progressives_____

_____

7. Traditionalists_____

_____

8. Tracking_____

_____

APPLICATIONS

For each of the following, fill in the blank with one of the terms listed above.

1. If a college admissions board were interested in assessing prospective students' general abilities, they would most likely require that the students take the _____.

2. An educator who believes that the purpose of school is to teach students math and science and how to read and write is a _____.

3. An adolescent who is concerned about the fate of society has shifted from egocentrism to _____.

4. The ability to discover problems and raise general questions about issues that are not well-defined is part of the proposed fifth stage of cognitive development, the _____ stage.

5. An adolescent's belief that she will not get into a car accident if she drives drunk is called the _____.

6. An educator who believes that the schools are responsible for teaching students about facets of life such as sex education and drug education is a _____.

7. An educator who is interested in assessing a child's knowledge of a specific subject such as social studies would most likely want the student to take the _____.

8. _____ is an organizational technique that permits schools to create homogeneous groupings of students within a heterogeneous student population in order to facilitate instruction of all students.

SELF-TEST MULTIPLE CHOICE QUESTIONS

Circle the best answer for each question.

1. Piaget's final stage of cognitive development is referred to as the
    a. preoperational stage.
    b. concrete operational stage.
    c. formal operational stage.
    d. problem-finding stage.

2. Piaget's pendulum problem was used to discover
    a. egocentric versus sociometric thinking.
    b. the existence of the personal fable.
    c. if they had reached the problem-finding stage.
    d. the strategies adolescents use in problem-solving.

3. Piaget found in his experiment in which adolescents were to determine what affected the oscillatory speed of a pendulum that adolescents showed which of the following characteristics?
    a. They set about their investigation in a haphazard fashion.
    b. They recorded the results accurately and objectively.
    c. They had difficulty drawing conclusions from the results.
    d. They formed illogical conclusions.

4. According to Piaget, all of the following are major aspects of formal thinking, *except*
   a. introspection.
   b. decentering.
   c. logical thinking.
   d. hypothetical reasoning.

5. What aspect of formal thinking involves going beyond the real to what is possible?
   a. introspection
   b. logical thinking
   c. abstract thinking
   d. hypothetical reasoning

6. Seventeen-year-old Mary volunteers 15 hours a week to work at a homeless shelter as she began to focus on others rather than on her inner self. Mary's attention has shifted from
   a. egocentrism to sociocentrism.
   b. the real to what is possible.
   c. the concrete to the abstract.
   d. deductive reasoning to inductive reasoning.

7. It has been suggested that adolescents have a particularly idealistic view of how the world should be because of their ability to
   a. distinguish what is real from what is possible.
   b. be flexible in their thinking.
   c. use deductive reasoning.
   d. use inductive reasoning.

8. An adolescent who preaches about how animals should have the same rights as humans yet wears leather and eats meat, may
   a. believe that the practice of ideals is more important than the general principle.
   b. understand the general principle involved, but may not realize that specific practices should be done to support the ideal.
   c. not understand the abstractions involved in idealistic thinking.
   d. believe that others are more moral.

9. An adolescent's egocentrism involves
   a. believing that other people are as concerned with his appearance and behavior as he is.
   b. not understanding that another person sees things from a different line of vision.
   c. believing that other people have the same thoughts as he does.
   d. All of the answers are correct.

10. Todd thinks that there is no need to use condoms during sex, because he thinks that there is no way he could ever get a sexually transmitted disease. Todd has constructed the
    a. personal fable.
    b. imaginary audience.
    c. foundling fantasy.
    d. adolescent myth.

11. Which of the following statements about creativity is *true*?
    a. Adolescents are too concerned with their own appearance to express much creativity.
    b. Adolescents are less creative because of their emphasis on logical thinking.
    c. Most adolescents tend to express more creativity as they get older.
    d. Adolescents tend to have more creative capabilities, but are less likely to express them because of increasing pressures to conform.

12. A fifth stage of cognitive development characterized by the ability to create, to discover, and to formulate problems is known as the
    a. abstraction stage.
    b. problem-solving stage.
    c. logical stage.
    d. hypothetical stage.

13. Some researchers have suggested that there is a stage beyond formal operations that some people reach that involves the ability to
    a. solve complex problems that are presented to them.
    b. be critical of material that is presented, rather than just accepting it as truth.
    c. reason abstractly and think of future possibilities.
    d. create and discover problems that have not already been delineated.

14. The SAT was designed to measure
    a. the general level of intelligence.
    b. specific knowledge that has been acquired in certain subject areas.
    c. the ability to engage in formal operational thinking and problem-solving.
    d. basic abilities that are acquired over a lifetime.

15. What is the maximum score for the SAT?
    a. 36
    b. 100
    c. 800
    d. 1600

16. Which of the following subjects is *not* included as an Academic Test on the ACT Assessment Program?
    a. science reasoning
    b. geography
    c. reading
    d. math

17. What is the maximum score for the ACT?
    a. 20
    b. 36
    c. 800
    d. 1600

18. Those who argue that the child's purpose for attending school is to learn math, science, history, and languages are considered
    a. traditionalists.
    b. authoritarian.
    c. authoritative.
    d. progressives.

19. An educator who argues that children should be enrolled in sex education classes because they are not getting the knowledge that they need at home would be considered a
    a. traditionalist.
    b. progressive.
    c. reformist.
    d. revolutionist.

20. In the 1950s, after the Soviet Union launched the first space satellite, the American school system
    a. took on a more progressive approach to schooling.
    b. revamped their system, particularly emphasizing revision of the math and sciences curricula.
    c. placed more emphasis on "hands on" experience.
    d. lowered graduation requirements so that more individuals could go on to college.

21. What was the overall school dropout rate in 1993?
    a. 4.6 percent
    b. 9.4 percent
    c. 15.2 percent
    d. 21.8 percent

22. What percent of American teenagers hold part-time jobs?
    a. 26 percent
    b. 48 percent
    c. 64 percent
    d. 80 percent

23. The parenting pattern among middle-class parents that is characterized by setting no consistent limits or standards and showing little interest is called
    a. conflicted parents.
    b. indifferent parents.
    c. overprotective parents,
    d. upward-striving parents.

24. Janice constantly criticizes and pressures her teenage son to get good marks. What parenting pattern may be contributing to his academic underachievement?
    a. conflicted parenting
    b. indifferent parenting
    c. overprotective parenting
    d. upward-striving parenting

25. What type of school integrates education, medical, social, and/or human services that are beneficial to children and their families on school grounds?
    a. Head Start programs
    b. full-service schools
    c. alternative schools
    d. community-based drop-in centers

THINKING CRITICALLY ABOUT YOUR DEVELOPMENT

Integrate material from the chapter with your own developmental experiences to respond to the following items.

1. Are you a formal operational thinker? Cite evidence that supports your answer.

2. Did you take the SAT or ACT before entering college? If so, were the test results predictive of your performance in college? What do you think are the best predictors of college success that admissions counselors should consider?

3. Did your elementary school and high school emphasize a progressive approach or a more traditional approach to education? Provide examples.

4. How did your middle school and junior high school help in the transition from elementary school to high school? Provide examples.

5. Which of the factors listed in the text were most important in enabling you to achieve academically? Explain.

ANSWER KEY

APPLICATIONS

1. Scholastic Assessment Test (SAT)
2. traditionalist
3. sociocentrism
4. problem-finding
5. personal fable
6. progressive
7. ACT Assessment Program
8. tracking

MULTIPLE CHOICE

1.	c	6.	a	11.	d	16.	b	21.	b
2.	d	7.	a	12.	b	17.	b	22.	d
3.	b	8.	b	13.	d	18.	a	23.	b
4.	b	9.	a	14.	d	19.	b	24.	d
5.	c	10.	a	15.	d	20.	b	25.	b

Chapter 13
EMOTIONAL DEVELOPMENT

CHAPTER OUTLINE & OVERVIEW

I. Adolescent's emotions

    A. The components of emotions
1. One's emotional state affects physical well-being and health.
2. Emotions are important because they affect behavior in relationships with others.
3. Emotions are important because they can be sources of pleasure, enjoyment, and satisfaction.

    B. Emotions during adolescence - The majority of adolescents maintain effectively positive relations with their parents and continue to be warmly engaged with their families.

    C. Joyous states - Whether or not children are joyous, happy, and loving will depend on the events around them and interactions with people. By the time that children reach adolescence, they already exhibit well-developed patterns of emotional responses.

    D. Inhibitory states
1. Fear - Generally, as children grow they lose some of their fears of material things and natural phenomena, but develop more fears relating to the self, and involving social relationships.
2. Phobias - A phobia is an irrational fear that exceeds normal proportions and has no basis in reality.
3. Worry and anxiety - These emotions are closely allied to fear, but they may arise from imagined unpleasant situations as well as from real causes.
    a. Some adolescents grow up in a worry-free environment; others grow up under conditions that cause constant worry and tension.
    b. Generalized anxiety disorder is when anxiety becomes so pervasive and tenacious that it interferes with normal functioning.

    E. Hostile states
1. Anger - Anger in adolescence has many causes, such as restrictions on social life, attacks on their ego or status, criticism, shaming, rejection, the actions of others, situations, or their own inability. Men tend to express their anger, whereas women are socialized to inhibit their anger.
2. Hatred - Hatred can be a more serious emotion than anger because it can persist over a longer period of time, and can be a result of repeated exposure to a particular person or persons. Hatred is difficult to suppress, and may be expressed through words or actions in violent ways.

II. Self-concept and self-esteem

   A. Definitions
      1. Self-concept is the view or impression people have of themselves which develops over a period of many years. The self becomes increasingly differentiated with age.
      2. Self-esteem is the value individuals place on the selves they perceive.

   B. Correlations - Self-esteem is related to relationships with others, emotional well-being, achievement, the goals that one sets, and acting out behavior, such as juvenile delinquency.

   C. Parental roles in development - The quality of parent-adolescent relationships is related to an adolescent's self-concept and self-esteem.

   D. Parental control and adolescent self-esteem - Parents who show interest and care, and who are democratic, combining firmness and emotional warmth, are more likely to have adolescents who have high self-esteem. And the degree of family happiness has been found to be related to individuals' levels of esteem.

   E. Divided families - There are a number of factors that mediate the influence of divorce on a growing child.

   F. Socioeconomic variables - Socioeconomic status has an inconsistent effect on self-esteem. Generally, students with higher SES have higher self-esteem than those with lower SES.

   G. Racial considerations - Self-esteem among Blacks has risen along with racial pride. The self-esteem of Blacks depends partly on the extent to which they have been exposed to white prejudices.

   H. Short-term and longitudinal changes - Self-esteem is lowest at around 12 years of age, and gradually stabilizes during adolescence.

III. Emotions and behavioral problems

   A. Drug abuse
      1. The most frequently used drugs in the United States are alcohol, tobacco, and marijuana, in that order.
      2. A physical addiction is a physical dependency. Psychological dependency is when there is an overpowering emotional need for a drug.
      3. Youth are trying drugs at younger ages.
      4. Five patterns of drug use may be identified: social-recreational use, experimental use, circumstantial-situational use, intensified drug use, and compulsive drug use.

5. There is a correlation between excessive drug use of adolescents and disturbed family relationships and personality problems. Other correlates include: disturbed peer relationships, loneliness, rebelliousness, depression, and more frequent and unprotected sex.

B. Delinquency
1. In 1998, of all persons arrested, 19 percent were juveniles.
2. Psychological causes of delinquency include emotional and personality factors.
3. Sociological causes include family background influences, SES, neighborhood and community influences, peer group involvement, affluence and hedonistic values, violence in our culture, cultural change and unrest, drinking and drug usage, and school performance.
4. Biological causes may play a role in delinquency.
5. A high percentage of juvenile crime is drug-related.
6. One way to prevent delinquency is to identify who is at risk for getting into trouble and plan intervention programs.

C. Running away
1. Over 700,000 youths, ages 10 to 17, run away from home annually.
2. Children who run away from home can be classified according to the degree of conflict with parents as runaway explorers, social pleasure seekers, runaway manipulators, runaway retreatists, and endangered runaways.
3. The simplest classification of runaways is to divide them into two groups: the running from and the running to groups.
4. The *National Runaway Youth Program* has promoted nationwide assistance to youths who are vulnerable to exploitation and to dangerous encounters.

LEARNING OBJECTIVES/STUDY QUESTIONS

After reading this chapter, you should be able to:

1. Discuss why emotions are important.

2. Describe the three categories of emotions:

    a. Joyous states -

    b. Inhibitory states -

    c. Hostile states -

3. Describe the four categories of sources of fear:

    a.

    b.

    c.

    d.

4. Describe phobias and worry and anxiety in adolescence.

5. Compare and contrast the hostile states of anger and hatred.

6. Describe the meaning of self and the importance of realistic self-concepts.

7. Describe the meaning of self-esteem and its importance.

8. Identify factors that are important to the development of a positive self-concept.

9. Discuss short-term and longitudinal changes in the esteem of adolescents.

10. Examine parental roles in the development of self-esteem in adolescents.

11. Identify commonly abused drugs.

12. Distinguish between physical addiction and psychological dependency.

13. Identify and define five patterns of drug use:

    a.

    b.

    c.

    d.

    e.

14. Discuss the three major categories of causes of delinquency:

    a. Psychological causes -

    b. Sociological causes -

    c. Biological causes -

15. Provide the classification system of different types of runaways according to the degree of conflict with parents.

KEY TERMS

In your own words, provide a definition for each of the following terms:

1. Emotion _____

   _____

2. Phobia _____

   _____

3. Self _____

   _____

4. Generalized anxiety disorder _____

   _____

5. Self-concept _____

   _____

6. Proprium _____

   _____

7. Physical addiction _____

   _____

8. Psychological dependency _____

   _____

9. Parricide _____

   _____

10. Patricide _____

    _____

11. Matricide _____

    _____

APPLICATIONS

For each of the following, fill in the blank with one of the terms listed above.

1. A state of consciousness that is felt as an integrated reaction of the total organism, accompanied by physiological arousal and results in behavioral responses is a(n) __emotion__.

2. A person who is chemically dependent on a drug can be said to have a __physical addiction__.

3. Whenever Jonathan is asked to answer a question in class, even if he knows the right answer, he becomes so nervous that he can't speak and he begins to sweat and tremble. He may have a __generalized anxiety disorder__.

4. A person's opinions of herself, whether good or bad, make up her __self-concept__.

5. The self's core of identity that is developing in time is referred to as the __proprium__.

6. The overall perception of one's personality, nature, and individuality is referred to as the __self__.

7. Andy has an excessive, uncontrollable fear of snakes, to the point where he cannot even look at a picture of a snake without trembling. Andy most likely has a __phobia__.

8. A person who is not chemically dependent on a drug, but nonetheless, still craves and needs it, has a __psychological dependency__.

9. Dan exploded in a fit of rage and he shot and killed his father. He has committed __patricide__.

10. The killing of one's mother or father, known as __parricide__, accounts for less than two percent of all homicides.

SELF-TEST MULTIPLE CHOICE QUESTIONS

Circle the best answer for each question.

1. Which of the following emotions is a hostile state?
    a. contempt
    b. regret
    c. disgust
    d. dread

2. Which of the following emotions would be considered an inhibitory emotion?
   a. affection
   b. fear
   c. anger
   d. jealousy

3. As a child, Nicole tended to be emotionally unresponsive and distant toward people she did not know well. As an adolescent in similar situations,
   a. she is likely to continue this same emotional pattern.
   b. it is difficult to predict how she would react since there is little continuity between childhood and adolescent patterns of emotional responses.
   c. she is likely to react in a hostile manner, since adolescents become more hostile after going through pubertal changes.
   d. she is most likely to now respond in a friendly, warm manner.

4. Which of the following fears is a child likely to outgrow during adolescence?
   a. fear of failure
   b. fear of rejection
   c. fear of public speaking
   d. fear of thunderstorms

5. Susan is afraid to go outside her home, resulting in a very handicapping phobia. What type of phobia does she have?
   a. agoraphobia
   b. acrophobia
   c. hydrophobia
   d. hematophobia

6. Worry and anxiety can be distinguished from fear because they
   a. are hostile states rather than inhibitory states.
   b. are pathological states rather than normal states.
   c. can arise from imaginary scenarios as well as real situations.
   d. are directed only at specific people.

7. An irrational fear that exceeds normal proportions and has no basis in reality is called a(n)
   a. phobia.
   b. obsession.
   c. compulsion.
   d. generalized anxiety disorder.

8. Janet worries about the smallest mishap, dreading that something terrible is going to happen. What is her illness?
   a. obsessive-compulsive disorder
   b. generalized anxiety disorder
   c. manic-depressive disorder
   d. personality disorder

9. Incidents that make adolescents angry
   a. most likely have to do with conflicts with their parents.
   b. most likely are social in nature.
   c. are more likely to be about objects than people.
   d. are the same sort of incidents that arouse fear in them.

10. A fight with her boyfriend made Mary feel badly about herself for a little while. In this case, which dimension of the self, as suggested by Strang, was affected?
    a. general self-concept
    b. temporary self-concept
    c. conceptualized ideal self
    d. pragmatic self

11. Curt pursues excellence to an unhealthy extreme. He pushes himself toward impossible goals and measures his own worth in terms of his accomplishments. His behavior exemplifies
    a. generalized anxiety disorder.
    b. agoraphobia.
    c. normal perfectionism.
    d. neurotic perfectionism.

12. Which of the following is a true statement about the relation between achievement and self-esteem?
    a. High self-esteem can contribute to success in school.
    b. Success in school can contribute to an individual having a positive self-concept.
    c. The relation between school achievement and the self-concept begins early on in school.
    d. All of the answers are correct.

13. A person's self-concept is most benefitted by
    a. overidentifying with the mother.
    b. overidentifying with the father.
    c. minimal parental identification.
    d. identifying closely with a parent, but not overidentifying with either parent.

14. Which of the following parents are most likely to have a child with high self-esteem?
    a. parents who are very restrictive and critical of their child
    b. parents who pressure their child to achieve in school
    c. parents who are firm and emotionally warm
    d. parents who are permissive

15. Children from minority groups are most likely to have low self-esteem if
    a. they have maintained close friendships.
    b. they have experienced white prejudices.
    c. their parents have high self-esteem.
    d. None of the answers is correct.

16. Which of the following children is most likely to have low self-esteem?
    a. an 8-year-old in elementary school
    b. a 12-year-old in elementary school
    c. a 12-year-old in junior high school
    d. a 16-year-old in high school

17. Often when Beth studies for exams, she takes stimulants to keep her awake so that she can study more. Her pattern of drug use would be classified as
    a. social-recreational.
    b. experimental.
    c. circumstantial-situational.
    d. intensified.

18. Joe drinks with his friends as a way to "hang out with the guys." What is his pattern of drug use?
    a. circumstantial-situational
    b. experimental
    c. social-recreational
    d. compulsive

19. What pattern of drug use involves using drugs at least once daily over a long period of time to achieve relief from a stressful situation?
    a. experimental
    b. compulsive
    c. intensified
    d. social-recreational

20. Which of the following may be a biological cause of juvenile delinquency?
    a. drug abuse
    b. a slow-responding autonomic nervous system
    c. a rapid-responding autonomic nervous system
    d. overly developed frontal lobes of the brain

21. What is the strongest single predictor of delinquency?
    a. mother-absent home
    b. father-absent home
    c. association with delinquent peers
    d. low socioeconomic status

22. Paula ran away from home because her parents set a very early curfew. She went out with her friends to a bar, and then slept over at a friend's house without telling anyone else of her whereabouts. She would be classified as which type of runaway?
    a. social pleasure seeker
    b. runaway manipulator
    c. runaway retreatist
    d. endangered runaway

23. Steven ran away from home because his parents set a very early curfew. He went to a section of town where it was very dangerous, but he refused to return home until his parents changed the curfew. He would be classified as a
    a. social pleasure seeker.
    b. runaway manipulator.
    c. runaway retreatist.
    d. endangered runaway.

24. What type of runaway leaves to escape abusive parents or stepparents?
    a. social pleasure seeker
    b. runaway manipulator
    c. runaway retreatist
    d. endangered runaway

25. What is the simplest classification of runaways?
    a. the one-time offender and the repeat offender
    b. the simple runaway and the complex runaway
    c. the running from and the running to
    d. the pleasure seeker and the pain avoider

THINKING CRITICALLY ABOUT YOUR DEVELOPMENT

Integrate material from the chapter with your own developmental experiences to respond to the following items.

1. Compare your level of self-esteem and the factors that influenced it during your first year in high school to the level of self-esteem that you are currently experiencing. Explain the role that the following factors played in the past and in the present: relationships with peers, emotional well-being, goals, acting-out behavior, parent adolescent relationship, and divided family.

2. In your own case, was there a correlation between parental control and adolescent self-esteem? Explain.

3. Which of the four categories of sources of fear seems the most worrisome to you personally? Why?

4. Do you tend to be perfectionistic? If so, is it normal or neurotic perfectionism? How did it evolve? What can you do to be less hard on yourself?

5. Which of the categories of causes of delinquency (psychological, sociological, or biological) seems the most powerful to you? Why?

ANSWER KEY

APPLICATIONS
1. emotion
2. physical addiction
3. generalized anxiety disorder
4. self-concept
5. proprium
6. self
7. phobia
8. psychological dependency
9. patricide
10. parricide

MULTIPLE CHOICE

1.	a	6.	c	11.	d	16.	c	21.	c
2.	b	7.	a	12.	d	17.	c	22.	a
3.	a	8.	b	13.	d	18.	b	23.	b
4.	d	9.	b	14.	c	19.	c	24.	d
5.	a	10.	b	15.	b	20.	b	25.	c

Chapter 14
SOCIAL DEVELOPMENT

CHAPTER OUTLINE & OVERVIEW

I. Adolescents in their families - The family is the chief socializing influence on adolescents.

    A. What adolescents expect of parents - Some of the things that adolescents have reported expecting of their parents are: reasonable freedom and privileges, faith, approval, willingness to communicate, parental concern and support, guidance, a happy home, and a good example.

    B. Parent-adolescent disagreements
        1. When disagreements occur, it usually is in one or more of the following areas: moral-ethical behavior, relationships with family members, academics, fulfilling responsibilities, social activities, and work outside the home.
        2. A number of factors relate to the focus and extent of conflict with parents, including the type of discipline that parents use, the SES of the family, the number of children in the family, the stage of development of the adolescent, and the gender of the adolescent.

    C. Relationships with siblings - Siblings often provide friendship and companionship if they are less than six years apart, but there can also be sibling rivalry, particularly in early adolescence.

II. Social relationships

    A. Friendships of young adolescents - Adolescents want emotional independence from their parents and more emotional fulfillment from friends, which can sometimes be disappointing.

    B. Heterosocial development - Both same-sex and opposite-sex friendships are important by simultaneously providing for many of the social needs of adolescents.

    C. Group involvement
        1. Finding acceptance in social groups becomes a powerful motivation in the lives of adolescents.
        2. Personal qualities and social skills such as the conversational ability, ability to empathize with others, and poise are the most important factors in social acceptance, although appearance and achievement play roles as well.
        3. Boys and girls acquire prestige through fairly similar means. There is a greater acceptance of girls in traditional "male" activity today.

        4. Although delinquent or antisocial behavior may be unacceptable in society as a whole, it may be received more favorably in some gangs or other groups.

    D. Dating
        1. Some of the purposes of dating are: to have fun, for friendships and affection, to maintain status, as a means of personal and social growth, to become more sex oriented, to find intimacy, and later, to find mates.
        2. The most frequently mentioned dating concerns for men are: communication, where to go and what to do on dates, and shyness.
        3. The most frequently mentioned dating concerns for women are: unwanted pressure to engage in sexual behavior, where to go and what to do on dates, and communication.

III. Premarital sexual behavior

    A. Sexual interests - Gradually young adolescents become interested not only in their own sexual development but also in the opposite sex.

    B. Masturbation - One of the common practices of adolescents is masturbation, which is a normal part of growing up and exploring one's sexuality.

    C. Premarital sexual intercourse – Studies show a rapid rise in the percentage of youths engaging in heavy petting and premarital sexual intercourse.

    D. Saying no
        1. In a study examining adolescents' competence for perceived ability at saying no to unwanted sex with a boyfriend or girlfriend, a majority of the adolescents believed that they would be able to say no.
        2. Several predictors for confidence in saying no to unwanted sex have been examined. Of all predictors, gender was the strongest.

    E. Use of contraceptives - Large numbers of adolescents do not use any form of birth control and thus are not protected against unwanted pregnancy.

    F. Potential problems
        1. The net increase in premarital sexual intercourse accompanied by a lack of efficient use of contraceptives has resulted in an increase in the incidence of out-of-wedlock pregnancies.
        2. Adolescents who are sexually active may be exposed to sexually transmitted diseases.
        3. In surveys taken of undergraduates, both males and females report a lot of unwanted sexual activity.

    G. Is sex becoming depersonalized? - The preferred sexual standard for youth has been permissiveness with affection. However, there is a significant number of adolescents today who engage in coitus without affection or commitment.

H. Adolescent marriage
   1. The median age at first marriage has been on the rise since the 1950s.
   2. Numerous studies indicate that the younger people are when married, the greater the chance of unhappy marriage and of divorce.
   3. The most influential motivations for adolescents to marry are: overly romantic views of marriage, social pressure, acceleration of adult sophistication, sexual stimulation and unwed pregnancy, and escape from personal problems.
   4. Many of the adjustments young couples must make are more difficult because of the immaturity of the couple.

IV. Development of moral judgment

   A. Lawrence Kohlberg - Kohlberg identified three major levels of development of moral judgment, each level with two types of motivation.
      1. At Level I, the premoral level, children respond to the definitions of good and bad provided by parental authority figures, and decisions are made on the basis of self-interest. Type 1 obeys rules to avoid punishment. Type 2 conforms to obtain rewards.
      2. At Level II, the level of morality of conventional role conformity, moral judgment is based on a desire to justify, support, and maintain the existing social structure. The child of Type 3 conforms to avoid disapproval of others. Type 4 conforms because of a desire to maintain law and order.
      3. At Level III, the level of morality of self-accepted moral principles, individuals accept democratically recognized principles of universal truths because they believe in these principles. Type 5 defines moral thinking in terms of general principles such as mutual obligations, contractual agreements, equity, human dignity, and individual rights. Type 6 is motivated to uphold universal principles of justice that are valid beyond existing laws, peer mores, or social conditions.
      4. Kohlberg believes that the stages are universal and moved through in succession.
      5. Research has revealed that not everyone reaches Level III.

   B. Carol Gilligan
      1. Gilligan suggested that females approach moral issues from a different perspective than males: women rely on an interpersonal network of care orientation, and men rely more heavily on a justice orientation.
      2. Gilligan proposed three levels of moral reasoning of women: At Level I, women are concerned with survival and self-interest. At Level II, the need to please others takes precedence over self-interest. At Level III, which many never attain, the concern is about the consequences for all, including themselves, in making decisions.

V. Work - An important part of socialization is to learn to work and hold responsible positions, although there is some concern that some adolescents may devote too much time to jobs and not enough time to school.

LEARNING OBJECTIVES/STUDY QUESTIONS

After reading this chapter, you should be able to:

1. Discuss what adolescents expect of their parents.

2. Describe the major sources of conflict between adolescents and their parents.

3. Describe the variables that affect parent-adolescent conflict.

4. Discuss adolescent-sibling relationships.

5. Discuss the importance of the following social relationships:

   a. Friendships -

   b. Heterosocial development -

   c. Group involvement -

6. List the functions of dating, and cite dating concerns.

7. Describe the present trends in the incidence of premarital sexual intercourse and in the use of contraceptives.

8. Discuss the issue of AIDS and other sexually transmitted diseases among adolescents.

9. Discuss the problem of unwanted sexual activity among adolescents.

10. Discuss adolescent marriages in terms of frequency, success rates, motivations, and problems of immaturity.

11. Describe Kohlberg's theory of the development of moral judgment.

12. Discuss Gilligan's theory of the moral development of women.

13. Discuss some of the issues involved in adolescent employment while still in school.

KEY TERMS

In your own words, provide a definition for each of the following terms:

1. Imaging_____

_____

2. Masturbation_____

_____

3. Coitus_____

_____

4. Premoral level_____

_____

5. Morality of conventional role conformity_____

_____

6. Morality of self-accepted moral principles_____

_____

APPLICATIONS

For each of the following, fill in the blank with one of the terms listed above.

1. Monica decided to help her friend cheat on a homework assignment because she believed that the friend would help her out at a later time. According to Kohlberg, Monica is at the _____ of moral judgment.

2. Ken is usually loud and tends to dominate conversations. However, when he went on a date with Leslie, he made an effort to speak more softly and listen to what she had to say. Ken was _____.

3. John actively fights against capital punishment because of his belief that it is wrong to kill under any circumstances. He is probably at Kohlberg's level of _____.

4. Another word for sexual intercourse is _____.

5. Ron chose to help out with a charitable event because he didn't want others to think that he was a selfish person. He is probably at Kohlberg's level of _____.

SELF-TEST MULTIPLE CHOICE QUESTIONS

Circle the best answer for each question.

1. What is the chief socializing influence on adolescents?
   a. peers
   b. **family** ✓
   c. teachers
   d. older students

2. Authoritative parents are
   a. demanding but not responsive.
   b. responsive but not demanding.
   c. **both responsive and demanding.** ✓
   d. neither responsive nor demanding.

3. Parents who are responsive but not demanding use what parenting style?
   a. **permissive** ✓
   b. authoritative
   c. authoritarian
   d. neglecting

4. Which of the following areas of disagreement is most common for adolescents and their parents to experience?
   a. conflict over relationships with other family members
   b. **conflict over social activities** ✓
   c. conflict over work outside the home
   d. conflict over responsibilities at home

5. In terms of their adolescent children, parents of low socioeconomic status tend to be more concerned than middle-class parents with
   a. **obedience.** ✓
   b. achievement.
   c. initiative.
   d. grades.

6. Optimal parenting is characterized by a combination of
   a. low control and low care.
   b. high control and low care.
   c. **low control and high care.** ✓
   d. high control and high care.

7. An adolescent's need to be involved in a social group is primarily motivated by
   a. **a desire to be accepted by others.** ✓
   b. a desire to have as many friends as possible.
   c. the need to avoid their parents.
   d. wanting to avoid dating.

8. A study which sought to identify dating problems found that the most frequently mentioned problems of the men were
   a. shyness.
   b. communication.
   c. where to go and what to do on dates.
   d. unwanted pressure to engage in sexual behavior.

9. A study which sought to identify dating problems found that the most frequently mentioned problems of the women were
   a. shyness.
   b. communication.
   c. where to go and what to do on dates.
   d. unwanted pressure to engage in sexual behavior.

10. When an adolescent first begins to sexually mature, interest in sexual matters usually initially focuses on
    a. individuals of the opposite sex.
    b. individuals of the same sex.
    c. one's own bodily changes.
    d. the parent of the opposite sex.

11. Which of the following is *not* a parental function?
    a. advocacy
    b. protection
    c. guidance
    d. control

12. What is the most popular method of birth control among adolescents who are sexually active and use birth control?
    a. the diaphragm
    b. withdrawal
    c. the pill
    d. condoms

13. Which of the following sexually transmitted diseases is the most common among adolescents?
    a. gonorrhea
    b. genital herpes
    c. syphilis
    d. chlamydial infections

14. Few cases of active AIDS are reported for adolescents because
    a. adolescents are less at risk for AIDS than are adults.
    b. the incubation period for AIDS may be from a few years up to ten years.
    c. adolescents are much less likely to report it than are adults.
    d. adolescents engage in less sexual behavior and have fewer problems with drugs than do adults.

15. What method did Kohlberg use to study moral development?
    a. moral dilemmas
    b. marble games
    c. turn-taking in board games
    d. observations of preschoolers

16. What is Kohlberg's first level of development of moral judgment?
    a. amoral level
    b. premoral level
    c. morality of self-accepted moral principles
    d. morality of conventional role conformity

17. If your morality is based on self-interest, you are at Kohlberg's level
    a. I.
    b. II.
    c. III.
    d. IV.

18. A child who decides not to steal a piece of candy from a store only because he is afraid that he would be caught would be at which of Kohlberg's developmental levels?
    a. Level I, type 1
    b. Level I, type 2
    c. Level II, type 3
    d. Level II, type 4

19. Margaret is rushing her husband Phil to the hospital after an accident at home. Their daughter Ann tells her to slow down and stop speeding because it is against the law to speed, even though her father needs medical attention. Ann's moral reasoning would put her at which of Kohlberg's levels?
    a. Level I, type 1
    b. Level I, type 2
    c. Level II, type 3
    d. Level II, type 4

20. Gilligan's major criticism of Kohlberg's studies of moral judgments is that
    a. he looked at adults rather than at adolescents.
    b. he initially studied only males.
    c. he only studied Americans.
    d. All of the answers are correct.

21. Who proposed a theory of moral development for women?
    a. Kohlberg
    b. Gilligan
    c. Piaget
    d. Erikson

22. According to Gilligan, women rely more on a(n) _____ than do males in making moral judgments.
    a. care orientation ✓
    b. justice orientation
    c. orientation towards themselves
    d. consideration of law and order

23. Gilligan's level of moral development that has to do with concern for the self and survival corresponds with Kohlberg's stage
    a. 1. ✓
    b. 3.
    c. 4.
    d. 5.

24. Sue began sacrificing her own preferences and became responsible for caring for her six children. She wonders whether she can remain true to herself while fulfilling her children's needs. At what level of morality is Sue operating?
    a. Level I
    b. Level II ✓
    c. Level III
    d. Level IV

25. Sharon decided to volunteer to organize a fund-raising event that no one else had the time for, even though she herself was extremely busy. She told herself that it was more important to help out than to take time for herself. She would be at which level of moral reasoning according to Gilligan?
    a. Level I
    b. Level II ✓
    c. Level III
    d. Level IV

THINKING CRITICALLY ABOUT YOUR DEVELOPMENT

Integrate material from the chapter with your own developmental experiences to respond to the following items.

1. During your adolescence, what did you expect from your parents? Were your expectations met? Explain.

2. During your adolescence, what were the major sources of conflict between you and your parents? Be specific.

3. In your opinion, which of the functions of dating listed in the text is the most significant? Why?

4. Think about a situation that you recently encountered that presented a moral dilemma to you. How did you resolve the dilemma (and what was the justification for your decision or action)? At what stage of Kohlberg's theory of moral development did you function? Assess the same situation according to Gilligan's theory of morality.

5. Did you work as an adolescent? Describe the positive and negative consequences of your work experience(s).

ANSWER KEY

APPLICATIONS

1. premoral level
2. imaging
3. morality of self-accepted moral principles
4. coitus
5. morality of conventional role conformity

MULTIPLE CHOICE

1.	b	6.	c	11.	d	16.	b	21.	b
2.	c	7.	a	12.	c	17.	c	22.	a
3.	a	8.	b	13.	d	18.	a	23.	a
4.	b	9.	d	14.	b	19.	d	24.	b
5.	a	10.	c	15.	a	20.	b	25.	b

Chapter 15
PERSPECTIVES ON ADULT DEVELOPMENT

CHAPTER OUTLINE & OVERVIEW

I. Demographics

    A. Age periods - In this book, adulthood has been divided into three age periods: early adulthood (the 20s and 30s), middle adulthood (the 40s and 50s), and late adulthood (age 60 and over).

    B. Population trends - The median age of the U.S. population continues to increase as life expectancy increases.

    C. Implications
        1. The depression and war-period babies succeeded as adults primarily because of their small numbers and superior opportunities, in contrast to the baby boomers, for whom there is much more competition for jobs.
        2. The dependency ratio, the number of dependents for each person in the labor force, will continue to increase.

    D. Some positive developments and challenges
        1. The divorce rate has leveled off and is decreasing slightly.
        2. The aging of the population has caused a shift from a youth-oriented culture to an adult-centered society.
        3. One challenge that remains is to alter our age-appropriate norms of behavior and make the necessary psychological adjustments to living a longer, more active life.
        4. Society needs a new orientation to the concept of who is old.

II. Meaning of adulthood

    A. Social dimensions - The primary meaning of adulthood is social, in that one is perceived as an adult by others.

    B. Biological dimensions - An adult can be defined as one who has attained full size and strength, but this is not adequate enough because many who would still be considered adolescents have achieved their full size.

    C. Emotional dimensions - Being an adult also includes emotional maturity, emotional stability, and functioning autonomously.

    D. Legal dimensions - Laws attempt to differentiate who should and should not be accorded adult rights and responsibilities. One problem of deciding adult status by law is that chronological age is not always the best determinant of capability.

III. Transition to adulthood

   A. Difficulties - Becoming an adult is a complicated process, especially in a pluralistic and highly industrialized society.

   B. Passages and rites - In our culture, numerous rites of passage take place before adulthood can be reached.

   C. Socialization
      1. Socialization involves learning and adopting the norms, values, expectations, and social roles required by a particular group.
      2. Part of socialization is anticipatory: preparing for certain tasks. At other times, resocialization is required.

IV. Developmental tasks

   A. The twenties and thirties
      1. Detaching oneself from parents, which may involve establishing a separate residence and achieving emotional autonomy, helps individuals form their personal identities.
      2. A major task of becoming a mature adult is developing the capacity to tolerate tensions and frustrations.
      3. Young adults are also involved in making an occupational commitment.
      4. According to Erikson, the chief psychosocial task is the achievement of intimacy.
      5. Young adults must learn to manage and maintain their own residences.
      6. Many young adults become parents and begin raising families.

   B. Middle age
      1. Physical changes require psychological adjustments and adjustments in lifestyle and health habits.
      2. Usually, middle age is the most fruitful period of professional and creative work.
      3. Participation in community life is essential for society's progress.
      4. Part of the developmental task is to let go of the responsibility and control of the children.
      5. Couples whose children have left home face the task of working out problems and becoming close again.
      6. Responsibility for providing assistance to aging parents may increase.
      7. Once children are independent, crossing of adult sex roles becomes more apparent.
      8. There is an increasing need for couple-centered activities and an increased interest in having fun, pursuing interests, and finding new meaning in life.
      9. According to Erikson, the chief psychosocial task of middle age is the realization of generativity.

C. Late adulthood
1. The task of staying physically healthy becomes more difficult.
2. Adequate income may be a problem.
3. Keeping one's own home may be important.
4. Older adults may feel a loss of status when they retire. It is helpful if they set new goals and are able to maintain a comfortable lifestyle.
5. Their challenge is to find meaningful relationships with others and to adjust to new family roles.
6. According to Erikson, the development of ego integrity is the chief psychosocial task of the final stage of life.

V. Theories of adult development over the life span

A. Gould - phases of life: Gould outlined seven phases of life, beginning at age 16, of the changes and adjustments required as people age.

B. Levinson - seasons of life
1. Based on a study with 40 men, Levinson proposed a model of adult development that included periods of relative stability interspersed with periods of transition at ages 22, 40, and 65.
2. Levinson contends that women have life stages similar to those experienced by men, but that women face more serious life problems than men.

C. Vaillant - adaptation to life
1. Vaillant conducted a longitudinal study of some of the "best and the brightest" white males.
2. He found that the quality of childhood environments was related to outcomes, but it was not the sole determinant of success; that negative traits during adolescence did not predict adult outcomes; and that achieving intimacy during young adulthood was important for later marital success.

D. Comparison and critique of studies
1. The age divisions in the three studies are purely arbitrary.
2. All three researchers described a period of transition between adolescence and early adulthood, and a mid-life crisis around age 40.
3. These studies involved only middle- and upper-middle-class segments of the population; therefore, these results may not be generalizable.

VI. Causes of change and transition

A. Normative-crisis model - This model describes human development in terms of a definite sequence of age-related biological, social, and emotional changes.

B. Timing-of-events model - This model suggests that development is not the result of a set plan or schedule of crises but is a result of the time in people's lives when important events take place.

VII. Personality through adulthood - According to the five-factor model, certain clusters of personality traits remain quite stable throughout adulthood: extraversion, agreeableness, conscientiousness, neuroticism, and openness/intellect.

LEARNING OBJECTIVES/STUDY QUESTIONS

After reading this chapter, you should be able to:

1. Discuss the demographics of adulthood and the implications for our society.

2. Describe the positive changes taking place in our society as a result of the aging of the population, and challenges that remain.

3. Summarize the social, biological, emotional, and legal dimensions of adulthood.

4. Discuss the difficulty of making the transition to adulthood in our society.

5. Summarize the developmental tasks of early, middle, and late adulthood.

    a. Early adulthood -

    b. Middle adulthood -

    c. Late adulthood -

6. Summarize the developmental theories of Gould, Levinson, and Vaillant.

    a. Gould -

    b. Levinson -

    c. Vaillant -

7. Critique the theories of Gould, Levinson, and Vaillant.

8. Discuss the normative-crises model describing change and transition in adult life.

9. Discuss the timing-of-events model that describes the changes and transitions that take place in adult life.

10. Summarize research findings on the stability of personality through adulthood.

KEY TERMS

In your own words, provide a definition for each of the following terms:

1. Baby boomers _____
_____

2. Dependency ratio _____
_____

3. Normative-crisis model _____
_____

4. Biological time clock _____
_____

5. Social clock _____
_____

6. Timing-of-events model _____
_____

7. Normative influences_____

_____

8. Nonnormative or idiosyncratic influences_____

_____

APPLICATIONS

For each of the following, fill in the blank with one of the terms listed above.

1. Both puberty and menopause are determined by a _____.

2. The model that suggests that important events in people's lives, such as marriage or divorce, are what stimulates development is the _____.

3. An individual born in 1952 would be considered a _____.

4. Denise is graduating from college at the age of 22 and she knows that she must look for a job. She has been planning for it for the past few years. This life event is considered a _____ influence.

5. In our society, the majority of individuals who attend college begin so in their late teens or early twenties, thus following a _____ clock.

6. An individual who believes that adult development can be described in terms of a sequence of age-related changes subscribes to a _____ model.

7. Eric was unexpectedly fired from his job at the age of 45, thus throwing his life into confusion. This would be considered a _____ influence.

8. If one wants a way to refer to how many people there are in the work force in comparison to how many people are being supported, one could use the _____.

SELF-TEST MULTIPLE CHOICE QUESTIONS

Circle the best answer for each question.

1. Middle adulthood refers to the age period of the
    a. 20s and 30s.
    b. 30s and 40s.
    c. 40s and 50s.
    d. 50s and 60s.

2. Baby boomers have had to compete more for jobs than did the previous generation because
   a. more jobs have become available due to advanced technology.
   b. more jobs became available after World War II.
   c. there are so many of them competing for jobs.
   d. of the degree of stability in the economy.

3. A dependency ratio of 1.4 means that
   a. there are on average 1.4 dependents for every person working.
   b. there are on average 1.4 people working for every person not working.
   c. for every married couple, there are on average 1.4 children.
   d. for every adult, there are on average 1.4 children.

4. The number of dependent persons for each person in the labor force defines
   a. labor ratio.
   b. economical ratio.
   c. dependency ratio.
   d. demographics.

5. Puberty is determined by a
   a. social clock.
   b. psychological clock.
   c. biological time clock.
   d. transitional clock.

6. Which of the following is a task of middle adulthood?
   a. achieving autonomy
   b. finding satisfaction and success in one's occupational career
   c. staying physically healthy and adjusting to limitations
   d. becoming a parent and rearing children

7. A high school graduation ceremony is an example of a(n)
   a. ritual.
   b. transition.
   c. landmark.
   d. rite of passage.

8. Which of the following is a developmental task of early adulthood?
   a. achieving autonomy
   b. finding satisfaction and success in one's occupational career
   c. staying physically healthy and adjusting to limitations
   d. finding new meaning in life

9. Which of the following is *not* a developmental task of late adulthood?
   a. maintaining identity and social status
   b. staying physically healthy and adjusting to limitations
   c. achieving integrity through acceptance of one's life
   d. revitalizing marriage

10. According to Erikson, the chief psychosocial task of early adulthood is
    a. the formation of personal identity.
    b. finding autonomy.
    c. the achievement of intimacy.
    d. finding a career.

11. According to Erikson, the chief psychosocial task of middle age is the
    a. realization of generativity.
    b. achievement of intimacy.
    c. development of ego integrity.
    d. achievement of identity.

12. Who proposed a model of adult development that includes periods of relative stability interspersed with periods of transition?
    a. Gould
    b. Vaillant
    c. Havighurst
    d. Levinson

13. According to Erikson, the chief psychosocial task of late adulthood is
    a. the development of intimacy.
    b. acceptance of retirement.
    c. the continuation of kinship relations.
    d. the development of ego integrity.

14. What includes the life review, being able to accept the facts of one's life without regret, and being able to face death without great fear?
    a. development of intimacy
    b. acceptance of retirement
    c. continuation of kinship relations
    d. development of ego integrity

15. According to Roger Gould, adults reach a settling-down stage between the ages of
    a. 22 to 29.
    b. 29 to 35.
    c. 35 to 43.
    d. 43 to 50.

16. According to Levinson, between ages 40 and 45, people move into a period called the
    a. midlife transition.
    b. top of the hill years.
    c. breadwinner years.
    d. family years.

17. According to Daniel Levinson,
    a. females go through a sequence of stages very similar to those experienced by males.
    b. females go through a sequence of stages very dissimilar to those experienced by males.
    c. females do not go through any stages at all.
    d. males do not go through any stages at all.

18. Based on Levinson's model of adult development, a person who is upset because he is intensely reexamining his life and who questions every aspect of his life is probably between the ages of
    a. 33 to 40.
    b. 40 to 45.
    c. 45 to 50.
    d. 50 to 55.

19. Vaillant found that
    a. mental illness during childhood predicted adult emotional illness.
    b. childhood environment was the sole determinant of adult success.
    c. negative traits during adolescence predicted the worst outcomes as adults.
    d. men with unhappy childhoods were more likely to become mentally ill.

20. Vaillant's study also found that the achievement of _____ is very important during young adulthood.
    a. a successful career
    b. intimacy
    c. autonomy from parents
    d. trust

21. A model that describes human development in terms of a sequence of age-related changes is a
    a. normative-crisis model.
    b. timing-of-events model.
    c. transitional stage model.
    d. stability model.

22. According to the timing-of-events model, which of the following is most likely to lead to a turning point in one's life?
    a. becoming 40 years old
    b. preparing for marriage
    c. planning to change one's job
    d. an unexpected job layoff

23. The timing of marriage is an example of a(n)
    a. psychological clock.
    b. transitional clock.
    c. social clock.
    d. biological time clock.

24. Becoming a grandparent is an example of a(n)
    a. psychological clock.
    b. transitional clock.
    c. *social clock.*
    d. biological time clock.

25. Levinson's theory is based on the
    a. life events model.
    b. *normative-crisis model.*
    c. stability model.
    d. personal growth model.

THINKING CRITICALLY ABOUT YOUR DEVELOPMENT

Integrate material from the chapter with your own developmental experiences to respond to the following items.

1. In your personal experience, how difficult was making the transition to early adulthood? Explain.

2. Provide personal examples of how the biological time clock and the social clock has affected you.

3. Describe the social, biological, emotional and legal dimensions of moving from adolescence to early adulthood.

4. Which of the nine developmental tasks of early adulthood listed in the text have you accomplished? Which have you not accomplished? Are the others worth accomplishing? If so, what has prevented you from accomplishing them?

5. What normative events and nonnormative events have impacted your development?

ANSWER KEY

APPLICATIONS

1. biological time clock
2. timing-of-events model
3. baby boomer
4. normative
5. social
6. normative-crisis
7. nonnormative or idiosyncratic
8. dependency ratio

MULTIPLE CHOICE

1. c
2. c
3. a
4. c
5. c
6. b
7. d
8. a
9. d
10. c
11. a
12. d
13. d
14. d
15. d
16. a
17. a
18. b
19. d
20. b
21. a
22. d
23. c
24. c
25. b

Chapter 16
PHYSICAL DEVELOPMENT

CHAPTER OUTLINE & OVERVIEW

I. Physical attractiveness, abilities, and fitness

   A. Growth and aging
   1. Sometime during the mid-20s, the human body is usually at the peak of its physical development.
   2. One characteristic of middle age is a growing awareness of personal mortality accompanying the first physical signs of aging.

   B. Robust aging
   1. Robust aging is referred to by various terms such as "successful aging," "productivity," and "vitality."
   2. Research on robust aging has led to the recognition that people who do not suffer any known illness or severe impairments can exhibit quite a range of levels of functioning.

   C. Attitudes of society
   1. Self-consciousness about one's changing physique is accentuated by society's attitudes, particularly for women.
   2. Generally speaking, our society accepts a double standard for men and women.

   D. Physical fitness and health
   1. Chronological age alone is a poor measure of physical conditioning or aging; the emphasis should be on functional age.
   2. In general, reaction time decreases from childhood to about age 20, remains constant until the mid-20s, and then slowly increases.
   3. Most of the decline in motor ability occurs after the 30s.
   4. With increased age, individuals have greater difficulty with gait adjustment.
   5. The potential of increases in strength remains until almost 30.
   6. The maximum work rate one can achieve without fatigue begins to decline at about 35.

   E. Exercise
   1. Exercise is one of the best ways to prevent ill health and maintain body fitness.
   2. About 29 percent of adults 18 year of age and older do not participate in any physical activity. Walking is the most popular and one of the best forms of exercise.
   3. One of the simplest measures of health and physical fitness is pulse rate, which goes up during exercise and indicates the intensity of exertion as well as one's fitness.

F. Diet and nutrition
1. Proper nutrition results in feelings of well-being, high energy levels to carry on daily activities, and maximum resistance to disease and fatigue.
2. The average adult in the United States is 20 or more pounds overweight. In order to lose weight, either exercise must be increased or caloric intake reduced, preferably both.
3. Adults may require special diets, for example, diets low in saturated fats and cholesterol, sodium, and sugar.

G. Rest and sleep
1. Sleeping habits change as one ages, and the rest received may not be adequate.
2. Insomnia may be caused by underlying biological predispositions, psychological factors, the use of drugs and alcohol, bad habits, and negative conditioning. The most effective insomnia treatment programs use a multidimensional approach.

H. Drug abuse
1. The greatest abusers of drugs are young adults between the ages of 18 and 25.
2. Studies indicate widespread drug abuse among the elderly who report taking them for medical reasons.
3. All kinds of drugs are potentially more harmful for older persons than for younger persons.
4. The greater the number of drugs taken, the greater the possibilities of adverse reactions.

II. Some bodily systems and their functioning

A. Nervous system
1. As aging progresses, brain weight declines, but this is due to a decline in size of brain cells, and not because of cell death.
2. The brain's efficiency depends primarily on the amount of blood and oxygen it receives.
3. The most widely accepted explanation for the slowing down of bodily functions with age is that nerve impulses are transmitted more slowly as people age.

B. Cardiovascular system
1. Changes in the heart and blood vessels cause a decline in the heart's pumping power and stroke volume.
2. The health of the heart depends partially on the health of the blood vessels that transport the blood.
3. Heart disease is the number one killer of the elderly.
4. Stroke is the major cause of adult disability in the United States; however, survival is more prevalent than ever before.

C. Respiratory system - Lung efficiency is reduced during aging due to a number of factors. Thus, the elderly cannot tolerate exercise as well. Various environmental factors can aggravate these changes that commonly accompany aging.

D. Gastrointestinal system - Problems with liver functioning and gall bladder trouble are common in old age.

E. Urinary system - Diseases of the kidney can be serious because poisons collect in the body if the kidneys function improperly.

F. Skeletal-dental systems
1. One of the most noticeable signs of advancing age is a change in stature and posture.
2. One important disease that affects the skeletal systems of the elderly is osteoarthritis.
3. Periodontal disease and tooth decay are primary reasons for tooth loss.

G. Reproductive system
1. Menopause - The cessation of menstruation takes place over a period of years.
2. Male climacteric - The decline in reproductive function in the male is generally a gradual process.

III. Human sexuality

A. Sexual relationships - Although the frequency of intercourse generally declines for married couples, most couples still maintain interest in sexual relations.

B. Homosexuality
1. Homosexuality refers to the sexual orientation of a person who is sexually attracted to a person of the same sex.
2. The two major theories which seek to explain the origins of homosexuality can be divided into two broad categories: biological factors and psychological causes.

C. Sexual dysfunction
1. Any malfunction of the human sexual response system is called sexual dysfunction.
2. Male sexual dysfunctions include inhibited sexual desire, ejaculatory inhibition, erectile dysfunction, and premature ejaculation.
3. Female sexual dysfunctions include general sexual dysfunction, orgasm dysfunction, vaginismus, and painful intercourse.

4. Physical and emotional factors can cause sexual dysfunctions. Most difficulties can be cleared up with proper help. The causes of sexual dysfunction may be grouped into six categories:
   a. Ignorance and lack of knowledge and understanding.
   b. Situational and environmental circumstances.
   c. Inadequate stimulation.
   d. Psychological blocks.
   e. Negative feelings toward one's partner or disturbance in the relationship.
   f. Physical abnormality, illness, surgery, or drugs.
5. There are four types of help:
   a. psychotherapy
   b. marriage counseling
   c. medical treatment
   d. sex therapy

IV. The senses and perception

   A. Visual acuity - Visual acuity reaches a maximum around age 20 and remains relatively constant to 40, then begins to decline.

   B. Hearing acuity - Hearing ability reaches its maximum around age 20.

   C. Taste and smell - The ability to perceive all four taste qualities declines in later life, although the decrement is small. There is also decline in olfactory function.

   D. Tactile sensitivity: touch, temperature, and pain - There is some decrease in tactile acuity with increasing age, but the loss is small.

   E. Thermoregulation - Older adults have more difficulty maintaining body temperature.

   F. Sense of balance - A maximum sense of balance is achieved between 40 and 50, followed by decline, and an increase in postural sway.

V. Biological aging

   A. Senescence - Senescence is a term used to describe biological aging.

   B. Theories of biological aging
      1. Hereditary theory - The theoretical length of life is hereditary.
      2. Cellular aging theory - Aging is programmed by the limited capacity of cells to replace themselves.
      3. Wear-and-tear theory - This theory emphasizes that the organism simply wears out.

4. Metabolic waste or clinker theory - Aging is caused by the accumulation of deleterious substances within various cells of the body.
5. Autoimmunity theory - This theory describes the process by which the body's immune system rejects its own tissues through the production of autoimmune antibodies.
6. Homeostatic imbalance theory - This theory emphasizes the gradual inability of the body to maintain vital physiological balances.
7. Mutation theory - This theory describes what happens when more and more body cells develop mutations.
8. Error theory - This theory is a variation of the mutation theory which includes the cumulative effects of a variety of mistakes that may occur.
9. No single theory adequately explains the complex events that occur in aging.

VI. Prolongevity

A. Possibilities - The term prolongevity describes deliberate efforts to extend the length of life by human action.

B. Implications - The goal of prolongevitists is not simply to increase the maximum life span, but to retard both disease and the aging process.

LEARNING OBJECTIVES/STUDY QUESTIONS

After reading this chapter, you should be able to:

1. Discuss when the human body is at the peak of physical development.

2. Discuss the self-consciousness about one's changing physique accentuated by society's attitudes that equate attractiveness with youthfulness.

3. Describe the meaning and some examples of ageism in our society.

4. Distinguish between chronological age and functional age.

5. Discuss the importance of exercise in maintaining body fitness and good health.

6. Discuss the importance of proper nutrition for good health and discuss diets suitable for adults.

7. Discuss the importance of adequate rest and sleep in maximizing healthful functioning and factors that contribute to insomnia.

8. Discuss patterns of drug abuse among adults.

9. Describe age-related changes and common diseases of the following systems:

   a. Nervous system -

   b. Cardiovascular system -

   c. Respiratory system -

   d. Gastrointestinal system -

   e. Urinary system -

   f. Skeletal-dental systems -

   g. Reproductive system -

10. Summarize the data on the incidence and frequency of marital sex.

11. Examine causes for homosexuality.

12. Discuss the different types of male and female sexual dysfunctions.

13. Describe age-related changes in the following sensory systems:

    a. Visual acuity -

    b. Hearing acuity -

    c. Taste -

    d. Smell -

    e. Tactile sensitivity -

14. Identify main theories of biological aging.

15. Distinguish between longevity and prolongevity, and state the goal of prolongevitists.

KEY TERMS I

In your own words, provide a definition for each of the following terms:

1. Ageism _____

2. Functional age _____

3. Reaction time _____

4. Motor ability _____

5. Pulse rate _____

6. Nutrient density _____

7. Basal calories _____

8. Activity calories _____

9. Saturated fats _____

10. Cholesterol _____

11. LDL (low-density lipoprotein) _____

12. HDL (high-density lipoprotein)_____

_____

13. Psychotropics_____

_____

14. Arteriosclerosis_____

_____

15. Systolic blood pressure_____

_____

16. Diastolic blood pressure_____

_____

17. Hypertensive heart disease_____

_____

18. Atherosclerosis_____

_____

19. Angina pectoris_____

_____

20. Coronary occlusion with myocardial infarction_____

_____

21. Ischemic heart disease_____

_____

22. Congestive heart failure_____

_____

APPLICATIONS I

For each of the following, fill in the blank with one of the terms listed above.

1. Calories metabolized by the body to carry on its physiological functions and maintain normal body temperature are _____.

2. The number of times the heart beats per minute is called the _____.

3. Harmful cholesterol is called _____.

4. The most common and serious diseases of the heart in the elderly are _____.

5. The time interval between hearing your name called and turning your head in the direction of the voice is called the _____.

6. Animal fats are also known as _____.

7. The pressure produced by the heart forcing out blood is called _____.

8. Television programs that portray older individuals as being irritable and demanding are engaging in _____.

9. The energy that is expended when an individual jogs is referred to as _____.

10. When a person suffers a complete cutoff of blood from a coronary artery, he has experienced a _____.

11. A person who is physically and mentally fit and is very active probably has a lower _____ than chronological age.

12. The hardening of the arteries by a buildup of calcium in the middle muscle layer of arterial tissue is called _____.

13. A candy bar that has few nutrients, but is high in calories, has a low _____.

14. Mood-altering drugs are called _____.

15. A type of heart disease caused by high blood pressure is called _____.

KEY TERMS II

In your own words, provide a definition for each of the following terms:

1. Edema _____

   _____

2. Cardiac arrhythmias _____

   _____

3. Cerebrovascular disease _____

   _____

4. Thrombosis _____

   _____

5. Embolism _____

   _____

6. Hemorrhage _____

   _____

7. Stroke _____

   _____

8. Pulmonary thrombosis _____

   _____

9. Pulmonary embolism _____

   _____

10. Vital capacity _____

    _____

11. Alveoli _____

    _____

12. Tuberculosis_____
_____

13. Bronchial pneumonia_____
_____

14. Pulmonary infections_____
_____

15. Emphysema_____
_____

16. Glycogen_____
_____

17. Pernicious anemia_____
_____

18. Hemoglobin_____
_____

19. Jaundice_____
_____

20. Cirrhosis_____
_____

21. Gallbladder trouble_____
_____

22. Bile_____
_____

23. Gallstones_____
_____

24. Insulin _____

_____

25. Diabetes melitis _____

_____

26. Gastritis _____

_____

27. Kidneys _____

_____

28. Incontinent _____

_____

APPLICATIONS II

For each of the following, fill in the blank with one of the terms listed above.

1. A condition characterized by buildup of fluid in the body is called _____.

2. A blockage from a blood clot is called an _____.

3. Irregularities in the normal heartbeat sequence are referred to as _____.

4. A person whose skin tissues turn yellow in color because of a liver infection has _____.

5. A blockage of blood vessels to the lungs by a blood clot is called a _____.

6. Stones that are formed in the gall bladder or bile passages when the bile becomes overconcentrated are called _____.

7. If the pancreas does not produce sufficient insulin, there may be excess sugar in the system and the individual may suffer from _____.

8. A person who has a blood vessel that ruptures, causing severe bleeding, is experiencing _____.

9. The volume of air inhaled by the lungs with each breath is called the _____.

10. When the body needs sugar, the liver releases _____ into the bloodstream.

11. The hormone secreted by the pancreas that regulates the blood sugar level is called _____.

12. When the connective tissue of the liver becomes hard, lumpy, and shriveled, the individual has _____.

13. A person who has a _____ may become paralyzed because the blood supply to part of the brain has been cut off and some brain cells have died.

14. The red pigment of the blood is called _____.

15. Inflammation of the stomach lining is called _____.

KEY TERMS III

In your own words, provide a definition for each of the following terms:

1. Osteoarthritis _____
   _____

2. Rheumatoid arthritis _____
   _____

3. Periodontal disease _____
   _____

4. Osteoporosis _____
   _____

5. Menopause _____
   _____

6. Climacteric _____
   _____

7. Sexual dysfunction_____
_____

8. Inhibited sexual desire_____
_____

9. Ejaculatory_____
_____

10. Erectile dysfunction_____
_____

11. Premature ejaculation_____
_____

12. General sexual dysfunction_____
_____

13. Orgasm dysfunction_____
_____

14. Vaginismus_____
_____

15. Dyspareunia_____
_____

16. Visual acuity_____
_____

17. Presbyopia_____
_____

18. Accommodation_____
_____

19. Adaptation_____

_____

20. Peripheral vision_____

_____

21. Cataracts_____

_____

22. Glaucoma_____

_____

23. Macular diseases_____

_____

24. Presbycusis_____

_____

25. Tactile acuity_____

_____

26. Thermoregulation_____

_____

27. Senescence_____

_____

APPLICATIONS III

For each of the following, fill in the blank with one of the terms listed above.

1. Even though the human body is exposed to many different external temperatures, we maintain a constant body temperature because we are capable of _____.

2. The term _____ refers to a man's middle years' changes as well as menopause or changes marking the transition from one stage of life to another.

3. A person who is able to see small details of an intricate map has good _____.

4. James is very frustrated because he cannot maintain an erection long enough to have intercourse. This is an example of _____.

5. A person with _____ may lose her vision over time because the fluid pressure within the eyeball increases.

6. A person whose lenses of the eyes are cloudy and opaque may have _____.

7. A middle-aged woman who has permanently ceased menstruating has gone through _____.

8. A male who is unable to reach a climax, even though he desires an orgasm and is stimulated enough to trigger a climax, suffers from _____.

9. Jane is unable to enjoy intercourse because she experiences spasms and contractions of her vaginal muscles. This is called _____.

10. A condition in which there is decalcification and loss of bone is called _____.

11. The ability of the eye to open and close the pupil depending on the amount of light is called _____.

12. Farsightedness is also known as _____.

13. The process of biological aging is called _____.

14. A person who chronically has painful swelling of the small joints in her hands and wrists and experiences disfigurement in her hands may have _____.

15. Any malfunction of the human sexual response system is termed _____.

SELF-TEST MULTIPLE CHOICE QUESTIONS

Circle the best answer for each question.

1. When is the human body at the peak of physical development?
   a. teen years
   b. mid-20s
   c. mid-30s
   d. mid-40s

2. When Marie visited her grandmother, she shouted at her, even though her grandmother is not hard of hearing. This is an example of
   a. ageism.
   b. transference.
   c. projection.
   d. rationalization.

3. The *double standard* as it relates to women and aging applies to
   a. mental health.
   b. retirement.
   c. employment.
   d. physical appearance.

4. A 50-year-old who acts like a 70-year-old has a higher _____ age than _____ age.
   a. mental; chronological
   b. chronological; mental
   c. functional; chronological
   d. chronological; functional

5. At what age is a person likely to have the fastest reaction time?
   a. 7 years old
   b. 13 years old
   c. 16 years old
   d. 25 years old

6. A person who plays basketball recreationally would most likely notice a decline in skills
   a. after turning 40.
   b. after turning 50.
   c. during the 20s.
   d. during the teens.

7. A blockage from any kind of undissolved material in the blood is called
   a. thrombosis.
   b. embolism.
   c. stroke.
   d. hemorrhage.

8. Victor is very physically fit and regularly exercises, while Mickey is not. If they go out running together, what will happen to their pulse rates?
   a. Mickey's will be higher than Victor's.
   b. Victor's will be higher than Mickey's.
   c. They will increase at the same rate because they are engaging in the same exercise.
   d. They will decrease at the same rate because they are engaging in the same exercise.

9. Adult diets should have food of greater nutrient density because
    a. adults require more calories with age.
    b. energy requirements decrease, but adults still need as many nutrients.
    c. nutritional needs decrease, but energy requirements increase.
    d. more calories and more nutrients are required.

10. Researchers who believe that people are biologically predisposed to insomnia suggest that insomniacs have
    a. overly active hypothalamuses.
    b. overly active hypnagogic systems.
    c. underactive arousal systems and overactive hypnagogic systems.
    d. overly active arousal systems and underactive hypnagogic systems.

11. With age, brain weight declines because
    a. cells die and are not replenished.
    b. nerves move closer together.
    c. the size of the brain cells decreases.
    d. larger cells die and are replaced by smaller, more efficient cells.

12. Bodily functions such as walking and writing slow down with age because
    a. nerve impulses are transmitted more slowly across nerve connections.
    b. the chemical transmitters deteriorate over time.
    c. the chemical transmitters change chemical structure over time.
    d. All of the answers are correct.

13. What type of heart trouble is caused by high blood pressure?
    a. atherosclerosis
    b. coronary occlusion with myocardial infarction
    c. hypertensive heart disease
    d. ischemic heart disease

14. Because the walls of the aorta become less elastic with age,
    a. systolic blood pressure naturally decreases.
    b. systolic blood pressure naturally increases.
    c. diastolic blood pressure naturally increases.
    d. diastolic blood pressure naturally decreases.

15. What is the number one killer of the elderly?
    a. cancer
    b. diabetes
    c. brain tumors
    d. heart disease

16. With age, the breathing rate _____, while breathing capacity _____.
    a. increases; decreases
    b. decreases; increases
    c. increases; remains constant
    d. remains constant; decreases

17. The gastrointestinal system includes all of the following, *except*
    a. kidneys.
    b. liver.
    c. pancreas.
    d. gallbladder.

18. What is the most important organ in digestion?
    a. stomach
    b. gall bladder
    c. liver
    d. pancreas

19. What is a major cause of cirrhosis of the liver?
    a. consumption of alcohol
    b. cigarette smoking
    c. air pollution
    d. All of the answers are correct.

20. Many older individuals become incontinent after having a stroke which means that they
    a. are paralyzed.
    b. are on a special diet.
    c. cannot control their bladder.
    d. are mentally impaired.

21. What is the end of menstruation called?
    a. climacteric
    b. menopause
    c. menarche
    d. amenorrhea

22. What disease is associated with the loss of bone mass?
    a. osteoporosis
    b. hypertension
    c. diabetes
    d. arteriosclerosis

23. Which of the following statements about menopause is true?
    a. Menopause is a disease which can be treated with medication.
    b. All women have gone through menopause by age 48.
    c. About 25 percent of menopausal women experience symptoms such as hot flashes, headaches, dizziness, joint pain, and bladder difficulties.
    d. Most symptoms of menopause are psychosomatic.

24. Ann, age 55, was told by her doctor that she has a buildup of pressure inside her eye due to excessive fluid. Ann has
    a. cataracts.
    b. myopia.
    c. presbyopia.
    d. glaucoma.

25. Harold, age 70, has just been told by the doctor that he has cloudy formations on the lens of his eye. The doctor referred to these formations as
    a. cataracts.
    b. glaucoma.
    c. a detached retina.
    d. senile macular degeneration.

26. Senescence, in contrast to senility,
    a. is a natural occurrence.
    b. is a disease.
    c. is not inevitable.
    d. None of the answers is correct.

27. According to which theory of aging is aging programmed by the limited capacity of cells to replace themselves?
    a. heredity theory
    b. cellular aging theory
    c. metabolic waste theory
    d. autoimmunity theory

28. According to which theory of aging is aging caused by the accumulation of deleterious substances within various cells of the body?
    a. wear-and-tear theory
    b. homeostatic imbalance theory
    c. mutation theory
    d. metabolic waste theory

THINKING CRITICALLY ABOUT YOUR DEVELOPMENT

Integrate material from the chapter with your own developmental experiences to respond to the following items.

1. As you get older, how difficult will it be to accept the fact that your body can no longer do the things it once did? Explain.

2. Were any concerns raised for you about your exercise, diet and nutrition, and amount of rest and sleep from reading this chapter? If so, list specific behaviors that you want to change.

3. Are you yourself ever guilty of ageism? Explain.

4. For you, personally, what is your functional age? Explain.

5. What habits do you have that are beneficial to your health? What habits are detrimental?

6. What is your attitude about body weight and about being overweight?

ANSWER KEY

APPLICATIONS I

1. basal calories
2. pulse rate
3. low-density cholesterol (LDL)
4. ischemic heart diseases
5. reaction time
6. saturated fats
7. systolic blood pressure
8. ageism
9. activity calories
10. coronary occlusion with myocardial infarction
11. functional age
12. arteriosclerosis
13. nutrient density
14. psychotropics
15. hypertensive heart disease

APPLICATIONS II

1. edema
2. embolism
3. cardiac arrhythmias
4. jaundice
5. pulmonary embolism
6. gallstones
7. diabetes melitis
8. hemorrhage
9. vital capacity
10. glycogen
11. insulin
12. cirrhosis
13. stroke
14. hemoglobin
15. gastritis

APPLICATIONS III

1. thermoregulation
2. climacteric
3. visual acuity
4. erectile dysfunction
5. glaucoma
6. cataracts
7. menopause
8. ejaculatory inhibition
9. vaginismus
10. osteoporosis
11. adaptation
12. presbyopia
13. senescence
14. rheumatoid arthritis
15. sexual dysfunction

MULTIPLE CHOICE

1. b
2. a
3. d
4. c
5. d
6. a
7. a
8. a
9. b
10. d
11. c
12. a
13. c
14. b
15. d
16. d
17. a
18. c
19. a
20. c
21. b
22. a
23. c
24. d
25. a
26. a
27. b
28. d

Chapter 17
COGNITIVE DEVELOPMENT

CHAPTER OUTLINE & OVERVIEW

I. Cognitive development

    A. Formal operational thinking
        1. Formal operational thinking involves the thought processes of introspection, abstract thinking, logical thinking, and hypothetical reasoning.
        2. Approximately half of the adult population may never attain the full stage of formal thinking, and some adults are better able to use formal thinking in their field of specialization but not in other fields.
        3. There is some evidence that older adults approach problems at a lower level of abstraction, but this may be because they approach problems differently.
        4. Older adults do poorly on measures of formal reasoning ability, but this is because they approach problems differently.

    B. Practical problem-solving abilities - Some research has found a diminution with age in capacity to do abstract problems, but an improvement in ability to solve practical problems that might actually be encountered.

    C. Comprehension
        1. Test of word familiarity have shown that adults generally show performance improvement through the 50s, after which scores decline. However, educational level was found to be more important than age itself.
        2. The ability to comprehend relativized sentences remains stable until the 60s, after which it declines.
        3. Older adults were able to comprehend the meanings of short prose passages almost as well as younger adults.

    D. Wisdom - One of the advantages of getting older is that people develop pragmatic knowledge we call wisdom.

    E. Problem finding - Cognitive growth in adulthood is continuous; there is no end point beyond which new structures may appear.

    F. Dialectical thinking - Some adults are better at an advanced form of thought called dialectical thinking, which involves being able to consider both sides of an issue simultaneously.

    G. Schaie's stages of adult cognitive development - Schaie identified five stages of acquiring knowledge and making increased use of it:
        1. Acquisitive stage

2. Achieving stage
3. Responsibility stage
4. Executive stage
5. Reintegrative stage

II. Intelligence

A. Scores on the WAIS as a function of age - The Wechsler Adult Intelligence Scale (WAIS) is the most widely used measure of adult intelligence. In general, verbal scores tend to hold up with increasing age, whereas performance scores tend to decline after the mid-20s.

B. Cross-sectional versus longitudinal measurements - Both longitudinal and cross sectional measurements show that verbal scores remain the most stable and performance scores decline the most.

C. Scores on the PMA as a function of age - Intellectual decline was less when measured longitudinally than cross-sectionally. Decline does not always occur, but when it does, it usually takes place after age 50.

D. Fluid and crystallized intelligence
1. Horn and Cattell found that fluid intelligence declined after age 14 with the sharpest decline in early adulthood, while crystallized intelligence showed increases through adulthood.
2. Schaie argued that the apparent decline in fluid intelligence was due to generational differences.

E. Criticisms
1. IQ is only one important factor necessary to carry out responsible tasks.
2. Some test items are more familiar to children or every young adults, and tests may show a cultural and economic bias.
3. IQ can be quite misleading. IQ does not measure innate capacity; it is adjusted for the individual's age.

F. Factors affecting scores
1. Adults score better if test items are relevant to their daily lives.
2. The complexity of the task, the degree of motivation, personality traits, physical factors, emotional factors, and hearing acuity can all affect performance.
3. The relationship between the test administrator and the test takers affects performance.
4. General intellectual level and years of school completed are related to test performance.

G. Personality, behavior, and mental abilities
1. There is a positive relation between mental health and cognitive ability.
2. Personality indirectly affects intellectual functioning by influencing life

cycle changes.
3. Individuals become more cautious with time, which may be related to test performance.
4. An individual with more intelligence and education will exhibit less rigidity.
5. The maintenance of intellectual abilities with advancing age partly depends on what people expect will happen.

H. Socioenvironmental effects
1. Older adults who are exposed to intellectually stimulating environments maintain a higher level of cognitive ability with increasing age than those who are not.
2. People with high education levels and superior socioeconomic status show less decline in cognitive abilities with age, especially verbal abilities.
3. Mental deterioration is also related to the frequency and intensity of people's life crises.
4. Abilities most dependent on acculturation are considered the most trainable.

I. Berlin Aging Study – Results of this study indicate that both sociobiographical factors and mental biological factors are significantly related to intelligence in general and to knowledge in particular.

III. Information processing

A. Memory
1. Memory can be divided into prospective memory (geared toward the future) and retrospective memory (memory for past events).
2. The three basic processes of memory are acquisition, storage, and retrieval.
3. Memory storage consists of sensory memory, short-term memory, and long-term memory.
4. Age-related differences in memory are not great.
5. Sensory memory abilities of older adults depend partially on the extent to which their sensory receptors are functioning at normal levels.
6. Tactual memory declines faster than visual or auditory memory.
7. Primary memory span does not change with age or it decreases only slightly.
8. Many studies show that older subjects perform less well than younger subjects when secondary memory is involved, but aging does not always bring memory deficits.
9. Older subjects are at their greatest disadvantage when materials to be learned are meaningless or unfamiliar, or cannot be associated with what is already known.
10. Facial recognition memory declines over age in adulthood as does memory for spatial information.

11. There are three kinds of long-term memory storage: procedural, semantic, and episodic. Age-related changes are found primarily in episodic memory.
12. In general, memory can achieve extremely high levels of accuracy, but people are sometimes susceptible to a variety of memory distortions and illusions. Several studies suggest that elderly adults may be especially prone to false memories.
13. Evidence indicates that memory of older adults can be improved with training.

B. Learning
1. Much of what was previously regarded as learning ability deficiency in later life is now seen as a problem in the ability to express learned information.
2. Verbal learning research uses paired-associate learning tasks, serial learning tasks, and divided-attention situations.
3. Motivation, which can be enhanced by relevance, meaning, and incentives, is important for successful learning.
4. The degree of association also affects learning.
5. Autonomic arousal is positively associated with serial learning at all ages, particularly for learning simpler tasks.
6. Older adults take more time to learn than do younger adults.
7. Some evidence indicates that there is a verbal learning deficit in the later years of life.

IV. Productivity and creativity

A. Creativity in late adulthood - Outstanding contributions have been made by many people during late adulthood.

B. Creativity as quality of production - Lehman found that in most fields people produced the greatest proportion of superior work during their 30s, although valuable contributions were made at all ages.

C. Creativity as quantity of work - Dennis, who looked at quantity of work, found that peak performance years occurred later than Lehman maintained, and that it varied depending on the field of endeavor.

D. Individual variations - Why individuals in the humanities remain creative into late adulthood, whereas the output of artists and scientists declines with age, remains a question. Certainly, individual variations exist in every field.

V. Education - Learning is a lifelong endeavor where there is no specific age at which people cease learning. And the concept of lifelong education is taken seriously today by educators and administrators.

LEARNING OBJECTIVES/STUDY QUESTIONS

After reading this chapter, you should be able to:

1. Discuss formal operational thinking and characteristics of thinking for adults.

2. Describe the practical problem-solving abilities of older adults.

3. Discuss the abilities of older adults to comprehend word meanings, sentences, and prose.

4. Define wisdom.

5. Discuss a possible fifth stage of cognitive development: a problem-finding stage.

6. Describe dialectical thinking.

7. Idenitfy and describe Schaie's stages of adult cognitive development.

   a.

   b.

   c.

   d.

   e.

8. Discuss adult intelligence and the changes in verbal scores and performance scores with age as measured on the WAIS.

9. Describe what happens to scores on the PMA test as people age.

10. Examine how fluid and crystallized intelligence change with age.

11. Summarize the criticisms of IQ tests.

12. Discuss factors affecting test scores.

13. Describe the relation between personality factors and intellectual functioning.

14. Discuss the relation between socioenvironmental factors and intellectual performance.

15. Summarize the findings of the Berlin Aging Study.

16. Describe the basic processes involved in memory and the three memory stores.

17. Describe the changes in the following types of memory with age:

    a. Sensory memory -

    b. Short-term memory -

    c. Long-term memory -

18. Describe the three kinds of long-term memory storage.

19. Describe the role of memory training in enhancing the memory of elderly adults.

20. Discuss the importance of motivation, relevance, meaning, associative strength, autonomic arousal, pacing, and speed in learning ability.

21. Describe the changes in learning ability with age.

22. Discuss creativity as quality and quantity of production and the changes that take place in creativity during adulthood.

KEY TERMS

In your own words, provide a definition for each of the following terms:

1. Field-independent people_____

2. Field-dependent people_____

3. Dialectical thinking_____

4. Thesis _____
   _____

5. Antithesis _____
   _____

6. Acquisition _____
   _____

7. Storage _____
   _____

8. Retrieval _____
   _____

9. Echoic memory _____
   _____

10. Iconic memory _____
    _____

11. Tactual memory _____
    _____

12. Primary memory _____
    _____

13. Secondary memory _____
    _____

14. Procedural memory _____
    _____

15. Semantic memory _____
    _____

16. Episodic memory_____

_____

17. Paired-associate learning_____

_____

18. Serial-learning tasks_____

_____

19. Intrinsic motivation_____

_____

20. Extrinsic motivation_____

_____

21. Associative strength_____

_____

22. Autonomic arousal_____

_____

23. Pacing_____

_____

APPLICATIONS

For each of the following, fill in the blank with one of the terms listed above.

1. Short-term memory is synonymous with _____.

2. _____ refers to the process by which acquired information is put away for later use.

3. All three sensory memory stores show some decline with age, but _____ memory declines the fastest.

4. "Dog" and "bone" are related to one another, therefore, they have high _____.

5. A memory of a song is part of _____ memory.

6. Motivation coming directly from physical and psychological needs is referred to as _____.

7. A person who tries hard at a task because he knows that he will get more money if he does well is working hard because of a(n) _____.

8. A person who believes in one opinion but is able to argue for the opposite point of view is able to engage in _____.

9. The process by which information is recorded, encoded, and stored is called _____.

10. Stored information is obtained either through recall or recognition in the process of _____.

11. A task in which a person is expected to learn a list of words in the same order that it is given is a _____.

12. The idea or point directly opposing a stated idea is called the _____.

13. A person who has rehearsed and learned a new telephone number has put that number into _____.

14. The memory of a person's face is part of the _____.

15. Memory of how to cook a grilled cheese sandwich is an example of _____ memory.

SELF-TEST MULTIPLE CHOICE QUESTIONS

Circle the best answer for each question.

1. A person who is able to sort out relevant from irrelevant information in solving problems is considered to be
   a. impulsive.
   b. reflective.
   c. field-dependent.
   d. field-independent.

2. Older adults, in contrast to younger adults, tend to be
   a. better at solving problems that involve abstraction.
   b. better at formal reasoning problems.
   c. better at solving practical problems.
   d. All of the answers are correct.

3. The ability to comprehend complex sentences
   a. remains stable until the 40s, after which it declines.
   b. remains stable until the 60s, after which it declines.
   c. continues to improve throughout the life-span.
   d. deteriorates slowly from early adulthood onward.

4. Some investigators have suggested that there is a stage beyond formal operations that involves the ability to
   a. discover new problems and raise questions about ill-defined problems.
   b. engage in abstract thinking.
   c. reason in a logical and systematic fashion.
   d. remember details from long ago.

5. Kim believes that capital punishment is morally wrong, yet she is able to consider that others disagree and she can present their side of the argument. Kim is able to engage in
   a. problem-solving.
   b. rational thinking.
   c. problem-finding.
   d. dialectical thinking.

6. According to Schaie, what is the first stage of acquiring and using knowledge?
   a. acquisitive stage
   b. responsibility stage
   c. executive stage
   d. achieving stage

7. In general, verbal scores on the WAIS tend to _____ with increasing age, and performance scores tend to _____.
   a. increase; decrease
   b. decrease; increase
   c. remain the same; decrease
   d. decrease; remain the same

8. Horn and Cattell found that _____ intelligence declined with age, while _____ intelligence increased through adulthood.
   a. verbal; performance
   b. performance; comprehension
   c. crystallized; fluid
   d. fluid; crystallized

9. Research studies comparing IQ scores at different ages may be misleading because
   a. IQ scores are dependent upon which age group the individual is in and are adjusted accordingly.
   b. IQ tests measure innate capacity which would not change over time.
   c. tests are designed for older rather than younger adults.
   d. variability is much greater among older individuals than among younger individuals.

10. Which of the following factors would be *most* likely to negatively affect test scores?
    a. high degree of motivation
    b. being physically fit
    c. having a cautious personality trait
    d. being self-confident

11. Which of the following individuals is the *least* likely to show a decline in cognitive abilities late in life?
    a. an individual who lives in an intellectually stimulating environment
    b. an individual with low socioeconomic status
    c. an individual with very little advanced education
    d. an individual with many life crises

12. Remembering to give someone a phone message is an example of
    a. iconic memory.
    b. echoic memory.
    c. prospective memory.
    d. retrospective memory.

13. Which of the following is *not* a basic process of memory?
    a. acquisition
    b. intelligence
    c. storage
    d. retrieval

14. Echoic is to _____ as iconic is to _____.
    a. visual; auditory
    b. auditory; visual
    c. tactual; olfactory
    d. olfactory; tactual

15. Primary memory is to _____ as secondary memory is to _____.
    a. short-term memory; long-term memory
    b. long-term memory; short-term memory
    c. sensory memory; long-term memory
    d. sensory memory; short-term memory

16. Jack calls the operator to obtain a phone number for a bakery. After he dials the number, he forgets it. This illustrates
    a. sensory memory.
    b. short-term memory.
    c. long-term memory.
    d. episodic memory.

17. Your birth date is kept in what type of memory?
    a. sensory memory
    b. short-term memory
    c. long-term memory
    d. episodic memory

18. Which of the following sensory memory stores shows the fastest decline with increasing age?
    a. visual
    b. auditory
    c. tactual
    d. olfactory

19. Which of the following is an example of primary memory?
    a. being able to remember the positioning of furniture in your house when you are somewhere else
    b. looking at a grocery list and trying to remember the first few items
    c. the ability to remember the faces of your immediate family members
    d. the ability to remember events that happened in your childhood

20. Elderly adults are more likely to have problems with _____ memory than with _____ memory.
    a. semantic; procedural
    b. semantic; episodic
    c. procedural; semantic
    d. episodic; procedural

21. Which of the following is an example of a paired-associate learning task?
    a. learning a list of pairs of previously unassociated words, and then being given one term from each pair and asked to remember the other one
    b. learning a list of words and recalling them in the same order
    c. remembering a list of words by associating each one with a word that is related
    d. learning a list of pairs of words that are related, and then being asked to recall both of them in the same order that they were originally given in

22. A person who is driven to learn because she wants to be successful at her chosen career is
    a. intrinsically motivated.
    b. extrinsically motivated.
    c. superficially motivated.
    d. relevantly motivated.

23. If a task is very complex, the level of autonomic arousal for elderly individuals is likely to be
    a. very high due to greater involvement, and thus they will perform better.
    b. very high due to anxiety, and thus they will perform more poorly.
    c. very low due to lack of involvement, and thus they will perform more poorly.
    d. very low due to lack of anxiety, and thus they will perform better.

24. Older adults are most likely to learn paired associates under which of the following conditions?
   a. if the words are presented four seconds apart
   b. if the words are sometimes presented two seconds apart and sometimes six seconds apart
   c. if they are allowed to go at their own pace
   d. if more time is given between learning the words and recalling them

25. According to Lehman, individuals in most fields produced their best works during their
   a. 20s.
   b. 30s.
   c. 40s.
   d. 50s.

THINKING CRITICALLY ABOUT YOUR DEVELOPMENT

Integrate material from the chapter with your own developmental experiences to respond to the following items.

1. Provide an example of an older adult you know who has "wisdom." Explain.

2. Provide an example of someone you know who is in Schaie's fifth stage of adult cognitive development. Explain.

3. Provide personal examples of intrinsic and extrinsic motivators to learn throughout your schooling.

4. Of the three kinds of long-term memory, which are you able to store most effectively? Provide personal examples of procedural, semantic, and episodic memories.

5. According to the text, age-related changes in memory are found primarily in episodic memory, with little or no differences found in either semantic or procedural memory. Provide an example of someone you know who fits this pattern. Explain.

ANSWER KEY

APPLICATIONS

1. primary memory
2. storage
3. tactual
4. associative strength
5. echoic
6. field-independent
7. intrinsic motivation
8. dialectical thinking
9. acquisition
10. retrieval
11. serial-learning task
12. antithesis
13. secondary memory
14. iconic memory
15. procedural

MULTIPLE CHOICE

1. d
2. c
3. b
4. a
5. d
6. a
7. c
8. d
9. a
10. c
11. a
12. c
13. b
14. b
15. a
16. b
17. c
18. c
19. b
20. d
21. a
22. a
23. b
24. c
25. b

Chapter 18
EMOTIONAL DEVELOPMENT

CHAPTER OUTLINE & OVERVIEW

I. Emotional maturity
   A. Emotional security – Being an emotionally secure person means having freedom from excessive, negative emotions and from crippling anxieties, doubts, and fears.
   B. Emotional stability – Emotional stability is a relative degree of freedom from drastic ups and downs of emotions.
   C. Capacity to feel – The emotionally mature person has the capacity to feel.

II. Subjective well-being - Subjective well-being can best be measured by indicators such as life satisfaction, morale, happiness, congruence, and affect.

   A. Life-satisfaction - Life satisfaction can be considered to have five dimensions: zest versus apathy, resolution and fortitude, congruence, self-concept, and mood tone.

   B. Sociodemographic factors
      1. Race - Negative effects of various physical impairments are stronger among blacks than among whites.
      2. Religion - Research suggests that the association between religion and well-being is consistent over the life course.
      3. Socioeconomic status - Satisfaction with one's financial status is more important in determining overall satisfaction than is SES by itself.
      4. Urban versus rural living - Urbanism influences life satisfaction indirectly and interactively because it influences health, financial satisfaction, and social integration, but overall, the effects of urban living on life satisfaction are inconsistent.
      5. Acculturation stress - Minority groups that move to the United States have special problems because of language barriers. Not knowing the language of the majority culture, they feels a sense of social isolation from the rest of society.

   C. Family relationships - Marital happiness is an important contributor to life satisfaction. Early relationships with parents also affect later well-being.

   D. Morale - The PGC Morale Scale evaluates three aspects of morale: agitation, dissatisfaction, and attitudes toward aging.

   E. Happiness - The young adult years are reported to be the happiest, but the present is reported to be a satisfying time of life as well.

   F. Congruence - Congruence begins with finding meaning in life, making sense, order, or coherence out of one's existence, having a purpose and then striving toward a goal or goals.

G. Affect - Affect, either positive or negative, has been found to be an important dimension of subjective well-being, and has both a hereditary and an environmental base.

H. Social networks - Subjective well-being has also been found to relate to the quality of social networks. Research has found that whether older persons had enough social ties in the objective sense was less important than whether they perceived that they had enough.

I. Health - Health is one of the most important factors related to subjective well-being.

J. Stability of subjective well-being - Research has found evidence of the stability of mean levels of psychological well-being in adulthood.

III. Stress

A. Meaning
1. Stress is physical, mental, or emotional strain caused by environmental, situational, or personal pressures and demands.
2. The amount of stress experienced depends not only on the severity and duration of exposure, but also on one's previous conditioning.

B. Causes
1. Job-related - Some stress is job-related. When the results of one's work are uncertain, stress is increased.
2. Role strain - Stress can result from role strain, when people feel that they can't manage their situations and feel in control.
3. Interpersonal relationships - Stress is likely to arise out of interpersonal relationships that are unpleasant and conflicting over a period of time.
4. Transition or change - Any kind of transition or change is also stressful for some people.
5. Life crises - Life crises, which are drastic changes in the course of events, can cause stress.
6. Self-induced stress - A great deal of stress if self-induced.

C. Effects of stress
1. The body goes through three stages in adapting to stress: an alarm reaction, a resistance stage, and then exhaustion.
2. Repeated stress can result in physical damage, decline in health, an increase in illness, and can interfere with psychological functioning.

D. Coping with stress
1. Coping strategies are conceptualized as either active or avoidant.
2. In a task-oriented approach, adults make a direct effort to alleviate the source of the stress.

3. Another approach to stress is a deliberate, cognitive effort to change one's internal responses.
4. Relaxation training is used widely to cope with stress.
5. Physical activity and exercise are useful for relieving stress.
6. Another way to deal with stress is to sublimate it through indirect means.
7. A common way of dealing with stress is to medicate it.
8. Increasing one's social interest and social supports can minimize stress.
9. Perceived self-efficacy is viewed as an important determinant of how much effort people will exert and how long they will persevere in the face of significant challenges.
10. Seeking social support helps in managing stress.
11. Hostile reactions to stress may or may not be helpful in relieving the stress.
12. Middle-aged and older adults tend to use more positive coping mechanisms than do adolescents or young adults.

IV. Patterns of family adjustment to crises

   A. First stage: definition and acceptance
      1. The first stage is the onset of the crisis and the increasing realization that a crisis has occurred.
      2. The first step involves defining the problem and gradually accepting that a crisis exists.

   B. Second stage: disorganization - During this period, the family's normal functioning is disrupted. Shock and disbelief may make it impossible to function at all or to think clearly.

   C. Third stage: reorganization - The third stage is one of gradual reorganization during which family members try to take remedial action.

LEARNING OBJECTIVES/STUDY QUESTIONS

After reading this chapter, you should be able to:

1. Identify and define the three components of emotional maturity.

2. Define subjective well-being and describe the specific indicators.

3. Discuss life satisfaction, its meaning, and the sociodemographic factors that correlate with it.

4. Discuss how family relationships influence subjective well-being of adults.

5. Describe morale as a component of life satisfaction.

6. Discuss happiness as a dimension of subjective well-being and discuss what research has found about happiness.

7. Define congruence and discuss its relation to subjective well-being.

8. Define affect and discuss its relation to subjective well-being.

9. Discuss the importance of both social networks and health as components of subjective well-being.

10. Examine the stability of subjective well-being.

11. Discuss the meaning of stress and its causes and efforts.

12. Describe some of the different ways in which adults cope with stress.

13. Identify and describe the three stages of adjustment to family crises.

   a.

   b.

   c.

KEY TERMS

In your own words, provide a definition for each of the following terms:

1. Emotional maturity _____

_____

2. General anxiety disorder _____

_____

3. Emotional stability _____

_____

4. Psychopath _____

_____

5. Subjective well-being _____

_____

6. Morale _____

_____

7. Happiness _____
_____

8. Congruence _____
_____

9. Affect _____
_____

10. Social networks _____
_____

11. Stress _____
_____

12. Type A personality _____
_____

13. Crisis _____
_____

14. Crisis overload _____
_____

15. Cognitive modification program _____
_____

16. Relaxation training _____
_____

17. Transcendental meditation _____
_____

APPLICATIONS

For each of the following, fill in the blank with one of the terms listed above.

1. A person with _____ is emotionally secure, stable, and has a capacity to feel emotion.

2. A mentally ill person who is incapable of the development of conscience or feelings for others is referred to as a _____.

3. Kim is very competitive, to the point of seeming hostile to her coworkers. She is always in a rush, and she reacts very strongly to stress. Kim can be said to have a _____ personality.

4. Losing a friend can be considered to be a life _____ because it is a change in a person's life and a turning point that will affect the future.

5. A person who is stressed can use _____ in order to relax the body.

6. Marcus, who has always wanted to be a doctor because he wants to help people, is currently attending medical school. His life, in terms of career goals, can be said to be high in _____.

7. Mary Jane looks back on her life and is very satisfied with what she has accomplished in terms of her career and her relationships with other people. Mary Jane possesses positive _____ well-being.

8. Peter, who is under considerable emotional strain both at work and at home, is experiencing a lot of _____.

9. Gary is in a program in which he is taught different ways of restructuring how he thinks about things, with an emphasis on positive thinking, in order to cope with the stress in his life. This type of program is a _____ program.

10. All in one week, Melanie's mother died, her child had to be hospitalized, and an important file was lost at her work. Melanie is experiencing a _____.

11. Lenny worries a lot and is agitated by little things. He is dissatisfied with his life and believes that it will only get worse as he gets older. Lenny has low _____.

12. _____ is a technique in which the individual tries to divert consciousness away from present troubling thoughts and toward a state of relaxation.

SELF-TEST MULTIPLE CHOICE QUESTIONS

Circle the best answer for each question.

1. Being free of excessive and crippling ups and downs of mood defines
   a. congruence.
   b. morale.
   c. emotional stability.
   d. emotional security.

2. A self-perceived positive feeling or state is referred to as
   a. morale.
   b. congruence.
   c. emotional stability.
   d. subjective well-being.

3. Which of the following is *not* a dimension of life satisfaction according to the *Life Satisfaction Index A*?
   a. congruence
   b. self-concept
   c. morale
   d. mood tone

4. Which of the following individuals is likely to feel the most satisfied with life?
   a. a person from a wealthier nation in comparison to someone from a poorer nation
   b. a person who feels he is better off than his closest relatives
   c. a person who has more children
   d. a person who makes a lot of money but wishes she were making more

5. What contributes the most to personal overall happiness?
   a. marital happiness
   b. satisfaction from work
   c. socioeconomic status
   d. social integration

6. Twin studies on the role of genetics in happiness and unhappiness indicate that
   a. a genetic predisposition for happiness runs in families.
   b. a genetic predisposition for unhappiness runs in families.
   c. a genetic predisposition for happiness and unhappiness runs in families.
   d. neither happiness nor unhappiness is inherited; it is a capacity that must be developed.

7. The *Philadelphia Geriatric Center Morale Scale* evaluates all of the following components of morale, *except*
    a. agitation.
    b. dissatisfaction.
    c. attitudes toward aging.
    d. incongruence.

8. A cognitive agreement between a person's desired goals and the goals that have been, or are being, attained in life is called
    a. affect.
    b. morale.
    c. congruence.
    d. happiness.

9. A survey by Chiriboga (1978) found that more people reported being the happiest during which period of their lives?
    a. teens
    b. 20s
    c. 30s
    d. 40s

10. The agreement between a person's desired goals and what has actually been attained is called
    a. congruence.
    b. life satisfaction.
    c. morale.
    d. happiness.

11. How is subjective well-being related to social networks?
    a. The person with the most social ties will be the happiest.
    b. The person who believes that she has enough social ties will be the most satisfied.
    c. The person who has his children nearby will be the most satisfied.
    d. The person who sees family members regularly will be the happiest.

12. Leeanne is a busy homemaker and mother with five children, who is constantly under pressure from family members to run errands, supervise children's activities, and maintain the home. She finds these demands stressful over time. Her stress results from
    a. life crises.
    b. transitions.
    c. rites of passage.
    d. role strain.

13. A personality characterized by intense competitiveness, hostility, overwork, and a sense of time urgency is known as having a
    a. Type A personality.
    b. Type B personality.
    c. Type C personality.
    d. Type E personality.

14. Sara is having difficulty coping with stress. Her unplanned pregnancy, her husband's recent heart attack, and a recent move have resulted in
    a. agitation.
    b. role strain.
    c. congruence.
    d. crisis overload.

15. What is the first stage in adapting to stress?
    a. resistance stage
    b. alarm reaction stage
    c. exhaustion stage
    d. coping stage

16. What is the final stage in adapting to stress?
    a. resistance stage
    b. alarm reaction stage
    c. exhaustion stage
    d. coping stage

17. John was a soldier in Vietnam. Today he still experiences terrifying nightmares and panic attacks as a result of his combat experiences. John suffers from
    a. senile dementia.
    b. dysthymic disorder.
    c. aphasia.
    d. post-traumatic stress syndrome.

18. Philip is feeling some stress because he just bought a new house and he is not sure he can really afford it. He deals with his stress by getting a second part-time job to tide him over until he feels financially secure. He has used what type of approach for dealing with stress?
    a. a cognitive approach
    b. a behavior modification approach
    c. a denial approach
    d. a task-oriented approach

19. Whenever Gail has to give an oral report at work, she feels a lot of anxiety and believes that she will do a poor job. She tells herself, "I'm no good at this; I shouldn't have this job anyway." Gail would probably benefit the most from which type of approach to coping with stress?
    a. a task-oriented approach
    b. a cognitive modification program
    c. relaxation training
    d. exercise

20. Which of the following is an example of using sublimation as a way of coping with stress?
    a. seeking out friends who will listen to problems
    b. becoming angry and trying to directly alleviate the problem
    c. becoming involved in enjoyable hobbies
    d. distancing yourself from the problem

21. A technique to direct one's consciousness away from thoughts and toward a state of relaxation is called
    a. relaxation training.
    b. avoidant coping.
    c. transcendental meditation.
    d. cognitive modification program.

22. During the first stage of adjustment to a family crisis,
    a. the family must define the problem and accept that it exists.
    b. the family is likely to become very disorganized.
    c. stress is at its maximum.
    d. family morale decreases rapidly.

23. During which period of adjustment to family crises are child and spousal abuse most likely to occur if it is going to occur at all?
    a. first stage
    b. second stage
    c. third stage
    d. fourth stage

24. To resolve a family crisis, the family must undergo a stage of
    a. disorganization.
    b. morale building.
    c. stress relaxation.
    d. reorganization.

25. At the end of a period of family crisis, the family
    a. returns to the same way they were before.
    b. is reorganized at a new level which may or may not be as satisfactory as the old one.
    c. will function at a higher level than before because they have experienced a crisis together.
    d. can never function as effectively as they did before.

THINKING CRITICALLY ABOUT YOUR DEVELOPMENT

Integrate material from the chapter with your own developmental experiences to respond to the following items.

1. Three components make up emotional maturity: being emotionally secure, being emotionally stable, and having the capacity to feel for others. Evaluate your own degree of emotional maturity based on the definitions provided.

2. How is your subjective well-being according to the Life Satisfaction Index A (LSIA) in the text?

3. Which of the methods listed in the text do you use to cope with stress? Explain.

4. Subjective well-being among older adults has been found to relate to the quality of social networks they maintain. Provide an example of an older adult you know who has successfully maintained these social supports.

5. Reflect on a family crisis from your past or present. What stages of adjustment did family members pass through?

ANSWER KEY

APPLICATIONS

1. emotional maturity
2. psychopath
3. Type A
4. crisis
5. relaxation training
6. congruence
7. subjective
8. stress
9. cognitive modification
10. crisis overload
11. morale
12. Transcendental meditation

MULTIPLE CHOICE

1.	c	6.	a	11.	b	16.	c	21.	c
2.	d	7.	d	12.	d	17.	d	22.	a
3.	c	8.	c	13.	a	18.	d	23.	b
4.	b	9.	b	14.	d	19.	b	24.	d
5.	a	10.	a	15.	b	20.	c	25.	b

Chapter 19
SOCIAL DEVELOPMENT

CHAPTER OUTLINE & OVERVIEW

I. Singlehood

    A. Marital status and delay - By age 45 to 54, only 8.6 percent of males and 7.1 percent of females have never been married.

    B. Typology of singles - Stein has developed a typology of single persons based on whether their status is stable or temporary, voluntary or involuntary.

    C. Advantages and disadvantages of being single
        1. Some reputed advantages of being single are: greater opportunities for self-development, opportunities to meet different people, economic independence, more sexual experience, freedom to control one's life, and more opportunities for career change and development.
        2. Some disadvantages are: loneliness and lack of companionship, economic hardship, feeling out of place in many social gatherings, sexual frustration, not having children, and prejudice against singles.

    D. Lifestyles - There are at least six lifestyle patterns of singles: professional, social, individualistic, activist, passive, and supportive.

    E. Living arrangements - Some of the different living arrangements of singles are: single communities, shared living spaces, living with parents, and living alone.

    F. Friendships and social life
        1. One of the greatest needs of single people is to develop interpersonal relationships that provide emotional fulfillment, companionship, and intimacy.
        2. Loneliness is a problem for a significant minority of never-marrieds.
        3. Singles have more time for optional activities.
        4. A greater percentage of married than never-married individuals report getting more fun out of life and that they were happy.

    G. Dating and courtship
        1. The most important element in attraction, at least in initial encounters, is physical attractiveness. Extroversion is considered attractive early on, and later, agreeableness and conscientiousness are important.
        2. One of the major problems of those who want to date is where and how to meet prospective partners.
        3. Male-female traditional roles in the dating process are changing rapidly.
        4. Although dating is usually an important part of the social life of young people, many haven't learned the social skills and developed the self-confidence to succeed.

H. Sexual behavior
1. According to one survey, 25 percent of never-married, noncohabiting men and women had no sex partners during the past 12 months. The findings present evidence that most people do, in fact, form a partnership and ultimately get married.
2. In general, almost half of men and women with multiple partners never use condoms. This finding places the sexually active people at high risk for AIDS.

II. Love and intimacy

A. Definitions of love
1. Love can be thought of as including these five elements: romantic love, erotic love, dependent love, friendship love, and altruistic love.
2. Sternberg described three components of close relationships: intimacy, passion, and decision/commitment. The most complete love, consummate love, is a combination of all three.

B. Mate selection
1. Some factors involved in mate selection are: propinquity, attraction, homogamy and heterogamy, and compatibility.
2. There is a filtering process of mate selection.

C. The older, never-married adult
1. The major difference between younger and older adults who have never married is that most younger singles consider their status temporary, whereas older singles are often well-adjusted to their situation.
2. The happiness of older adults is very dependent on satisfaction with their level of living and with their level of activity rather than just on the extent of social contacts.

III. Marriage and family living

A. Marriage and personal happiness - Marital happiness contributes more to personal global happiness than does any other kind of satisfaction, including satisfaction from work.

B. The family life cycle
1. The family life cycle divides the family experience into phases or stages over the life-span and seeks to describe changes in family structure and composition during each stage.
2. The general trend is for marital satisfaction to be somewhat curvilinear - to be high at the time of marriage, lowest during the child-rearing years, and higher again after the youngest child has passed beyond the teens.

C. Adjustments early in marriage - All couples are faced with marital adjustment tasks in which they try to modify their behavior and relationship to achieve the greatest degree of satisfaction with a minimum degree of frustration.

D. Adjustments to parenthood - The more stressful a couple's marriage before parenthood, the more likely it is that they will have difficulty in adjusting to the first child. Stress will vary depending on whether the child was planned and on the child's temperament.

E. Voluntary childlessness - The vast majority of couples want to have children, but voluntary childlessness is increasing, and society is more accepting of this life-style.

F. Adjustments during middle adulthood
   1. A growing awareness that years are numbered creates a sense of urgency for many middle-agers.
   2. For some, middle age can become a time for revitalizing a tired marriage, for rethinking their relationship, and for deciding that they want to share many things in life together.
   3. Some couples have trouble adjusting to the empty-nest years, but many are relieved and excited when the last child leaves. These years may be happier than earlier and later years.

G. Adjustments during late adulthood
   1. As health and longevity of the elderly increases, an increasing proportion of elderly adults are still living with their spouse.
   2. For many, marital happiness and satisfaction increase during a second honeymoon stage after the children have left home and after retirement.
   3. Sometimes during the last stages of old age, marital satisfaction again declines.
   4. There is some evidence that there is a reversal of sex roles in relation to authority in the family as people get older.
   5. Most older people are not isolated from their adult children.

H. Widowhood - The greater longevity of women means that the number of widows exceeds widowers at all levels. It is helpful to be able to maintain intimate relationships with friends.

I. Divorce
   1. Divorce rates increased steadily from 1958 until 1979, and have since leveled off and even declined.
   2. Marriage and family therapists have identified ten areas as having the most damaging effect on marital relationships, with communication problems ranked as the most damaging.
   3. The decline of intimacy and love, called disaffection, is a major component in the divorce process.

J. Alternatives to divorce - Before divorcing, couples may consider marriage counseling, marriage enrichment programs, separation, and reconciliation.

K. Adult adjustments after divorce - Some of the adjustments to be made after divorce are: getting over the emotional trauma, dealing with society's attitudes, loneliness and social readjustment, finances, realignment of responsibilities, sexual readjustments, contacts with ex-spouse, kinship interaction, and reconciliation.

L. Remarriage - Adults who remarry after divorce have some real advantages over those married for the first time, but for some, remarriage introduces new complications.

IV. Work and careers

A. Career establishment
1. Two major psychosocial tasks of early adulthood are to mold an identity and to choose and consolidate a career.
2. Discontentment with jobs or money affects other aspects of life.
3. Adults have been grouped into five categories depending on the status of their vocational development: vocational achievers, vocationally frustrated, non-committed, vocational opportunists, and social dropouts.

B. Women's careers
1. One of the most important considerations in the life satisfaction of working wives is whether they have been able to integrate their home life and their work life, and whether or not there is conflict between their family and job roles. Sources of stress include: the presence of young children in the family, the job itself, and the strain of having too many roles to fulfill at once.
2. Dual careers can create more stress, but can also be very rewarding. There are some important issues for dual-career couples: moving, travel, child care, household responsibilities and roles, scheduling, and identity and competitiveness.

C. Mid-life careers and employment
1. For most people, middle adulthood is the fruition of a long period of professional work.
2. When a person is shut out of a career or at a dead end, one answer is to begin a second career.
3. Although the middle years can be productive and rewarding for some, for others, they can be years of upset and anxiety.

D. The older worker
1. Most research has found that job satisfaction tends to increase with the worker's age.

2. The numbers of older workers in the work force may increase in the years ahead.
3. Forced retirement has been ranked among the top 10 crises in terms of the amount of stress it causes the individual.

V. Social-psychological theories of aging

A. Disengagement theory
1. This theory states that as people approach old age, they have a natural tendency to withdraw socially and psychologically from the environment, thereby freeing them from various responsibilities, allowing them more time and enhancing their life satisfaction.
2. Critics argue that disengagement is not universal, inevitable, or inherent in the aging process, nor does it consider individual differences in health and personality that influence activity.

B. Activity theory
1. This theory suggests that an active lifestyle will have a positive effect on the sense of well-being and satisfaction of older people.
2. Critics argue that the theory is oversimplified and does not consider those who cannot be active.

C. Personality and lifestyle theory - In order to study individual differences, some gerontologists have considered different personality types, such as: integrated, armored-defended, passive-dependent, and unintegrated.

D. Exchange theory - According to this theory, persons with the greatest needs lose the most power and those supplying needs gain power.

E. Social reconstruction theory - This theory states that our society brings about role loss for the elderly, then labels them negatively and deprives them of opportunities, leading to acceptance of the external labeling.

F. Which theory? - Each of these theories contributes something to the total understanding of the aging process.

LEARNING OBJECTIVES/STUDY QUESTIONS

After reading this chapter, you should be able to:

1. Discuss the incidence of singlehood and the four categories of single persons.

2. Discuss both the advantages and disadvantages of being single.

3. Describe the lifestyles and living arrangements of singles.

4. Discuss friendships and social life, dating and courtship, and sexual behavior of singles.

5. Identify and describe five different types of love.

   a.

   b.

   c.

   d.

   e.

6. Describe Sternberg's three components of love.

7. Explain the filtering process of mate selection.

8. Discuss the situations of older, never-married adults.

9. Discuss the relation between marriage and personal happiness.

10. Outline the stages of the family life cycle.

11. Discuss how marital satisfaction changes over various phases of the family life cycle.

12. Summarize common adjustments early in marriage.

13. Discuss the adjustments to parenthood.

14. Describe adjustments during middle adulthood.

15. Describe adjustments during late adulthood.

16. Discuss the incidence of divorce and the problems that lead to divorce.

17. Examine the alternatives to divorce.

18. List problems of adjustment after divorce.

19. Describe some advantages and problems of remarriage.

20. Summarize the process of career establishment.

21. Discuss some of the issues involved for women choosing careers.

22. Discuss mid-life careers and employment.

23. Discuss issues in relation to the older worker and retirement.

24. Briefly explain the social-psychological theories of aging.

   a. Disengagement theory -

   b. Activity theory -

   c. Personality and lifestyle theory -

   d. Exchange theory -

   e. Social reconstruction theory -

KEY TERMS

In your own words, provide a definition for each of the following terms:

1. Cohabitation

2. Date rape

3. Romantic love

4. Erotic love

5. Dependent love

6. Friendship love

7. Altruistic love _____
_____

8. Consummate love _____
_____

9. Homogamy _____
_____

10. Heterogamy _____
_____

11. Family life cycle _____
_____

12. Marital adjustment tasks _____
_____

13. Postparental years _____
_____

14. Misogynist _____
_____

15. Marriage enrichment programs _____
_____

16. Structured separation _____
_____

17. Burnout _____
_____

18. Disengagement theory _____
_____

19. Activity theory_____

20. Personality and lifestyle theory_____

21. Exchange theory_____

22. Social reconstruction theory_____

APPLICATIONS

For each of the following, fill in the blank with one of the terms listed above.

1. According to _____ theory, the people that are most dependent lose the most power, while those who meet those needs gain the power.

2. According to _____ theory, aging people naturally withdraw from society, and in so doing, they free themselves of many responsibilities.

3. The idea that society affects the self-concept of the elderly by having certain expectations is part of the _____ theory.

4. Diane and Tom live together with two children and are not married. Their living arrangement is that of _____.

5. When Sue and Ed's last child leaves for college and before they retire, they will be in the _____.

6. Ruth married a man who was very similar to her in terms of background, habits, interests, and likes and dislikes. This is an example of _____.

7. Rene and her husband enjoy participating in the same activities and enjoy being with one another. They have _____ love.

8. Barry has been working at his job for many years and recently has felt emotionally and physically exhausted from the pressure. He is suffering from _____.

9. Jack and Hillary go out on a date and return to her apartment afterwards. They kiss and pet for awhile, and then Jack forces Hillary to have intercourse even though she told him she did not want to have sex. This is an example of _____.

10. The _____ describes the stages and changes in family structure, and the challenges and tasks that the family faces over the life-span.

11. The theory which states that an elderly person who continues to be active will have a more positive outlook on life is the _____ theory.

12. The theory that considers the relation between personality types, such as passive dependent types, and patterns of aging is the _____ theory.

13. Mary and Lou have emotionally bonded, are passionate in their lovemaking, and are committed to each other. According to Sternberg, they have _____ love.

14. Lateka is deeply concerned about her husband. She enjoys caring for him and giving to him. She feels _____ love.

15. Timothy is extremely attracted to Vicki. He feels _____ love toward Vicki.

SELF-TEST MULTIPLE CHOICE QUESTIONS

Circle the best answer for each question.

1. Maria has never been married, but she would like to be and is actively looking for a mate. She would be classified as a(n)
    a. voluntary temporary single.
    b. voluntary stable single.
    c. involuntary temporary single.
    d. involuntary stable single.

2. Fred is single and a doctor. His major concern in life is his work, and he organizes his social life around his work. Fred would be classified as having what type of single lifestyle pattern?
    a. professional
    b. social
    c. individualistic
    d. passive

3. Shari is single and not much interested in pursuing an active social life. Instead, she enjoys her hobbies and spends a lot of time alone, enjoying her freedom and doing the things she likes to do best. She would be classified as having what type of single lifestyle pattern?
   a. supportive
   b. passive
   c. activist
   d. individualistic

4. Research suggests that the most important factor in attraction in initial encounters is
   a. extraversion.
   b. agreeableness.
   c. physical attractiveness.
   d. emotional stability.

5. What element of love is defined as sexual attraction to another person?
   a. erotic love
   b. dependent love
   c. altruistic love
   d. romantic love

6. A profoundly tender or passionate affection for another person defines
   a. romantic love.
   b. dependent love.
   c. altruistic love.
   d. erotic love.

7. According to Sternberg, romantic love is missing
   a. passion.
   b. intimacy.
   c. commitment.
   d. intimacy and commitment.

8. Sternberg's companionate love is made up of
   a. intimacy and passion.
   b. intimacy and commitment.
   c. passion and commitment.
   d. a balanced match of intimacy, passion, and commitment.

9. The major difference between younger and older adults who have never married is that
   a. most younger adults are happy with their situation, whereas the older adults tend to be more dissatisfied.
   b. most younger singles consider their status temporary, whereas older adults tend to be more adjusted to their status.
   c. younger adults tend to be more sexually active than older singles.
   d. older singles tend to be happier with their situation than do younger singles.

10. In general, marital satisfaction tends to be lowest
    a. within the first few months of marriage.
    b. before having children.
    c. during the child-bearing years.
    d. after the last child leaves home.

11. Adjustment to parenthood can be particularly difficult
    a. if the pregnancy was not planned.
    b. because the transition is quite abrupt.
    c. if the child has a difficult temperament.
    d. All of the answers are correct.

12. Research suggests that adults in the postparental period tend to be
    a. extremely depressed because their children have left.
    b. confused as to their new roles.
    c. happier than those that are younger or older.
    d. more unhappy with their marriages.

13. What factor have adults rated as the *most* damaging to marriages?
    a. lack of communication
    b. unrealistic expectations of marriage or spouse
    c. power struggles
    d. serious individual problems

14. Which of the following statements about divorce rates is *true*?
    a. Divorce rates declined from 1958 until 1979, and then increased.
    b. Divorce rates have increased steadily from 1958 to today.
    c. Divorce rates increased steadily from 1958 until 1979, after which they leveled off and even declined.
    d. Divorce rates increased steadily from 1950 until 1979, after which they leveled off but increased again since 1990.

15. During which phase of the process of marital disaffection are the partners optimistic about their future marriage?
    a. beginning
    b. middle
    c. end
    d. None of the answers is correct.

16. Marriage enrichment programs are best entered
    a. when one spouse wants to participate but the other one does not.
    b. before problems have become unmanageable.
    c. when the relationship has deteriorated to a point where it is difficult for them to solve problems.
    d. if the couple wants to reunite after a divorce.

17. Rebecca has just completed her M.B.A. and is looking forward to her new job with a prestigious advertising agency. She would be classified as
    a. a vocational achiever.
    b. vocationally frustrated.
    c. noncommitted.
    d. a vocational opportunist.

18. Jacob isn't really sure what he wants to do for a career. He has had a number of different jobs, and now he has taken a job at his uncle's company until he can find something better. He would be classified as
    a. vocationally frustrated.
    b. a vocational opportunist.
    c. noncommitted.
    d. a social dropout.

19. Whether or not retirement causes a lot of stress depends primarily upon whether
    a. their adult children are willing to support them.
    b. they had a choice.
    c. they felt they had performed well at their job.
    d. they have a second career, even if part-time, in mind.

20. Which of the following theories suggests that as people enter old age, there is a natural tendency to withdraw socially and psychologically?
    a. disengagement theory
    b. activity theory
    c. personality and lifestyle theory
    d. exchange theory

21. Which of the following theories is the most focused toward individual differences?
    a. disengagement theory
    b. personality and lifestyle theory
    c. exchange theory
    d. social reconstruction theory

22. Marty is afraid of growing old so he works very hard in order to maintain a lifestyle such as he had when he was a little bit younger. He believes that this will keep him from aging. Marty would most likely be classified as having which personality type?
    a. integrated: reorganized
    b. integrated: focused
    c. armored-defended: holding on
    d. armored-defended: constricted

23. In his older years, Will has become very dependent, but he is basically satisfied because his younger son attends to his needs. Which personality type is Will?
    a. armored-defended: constricted
    b. unintegrated
    c. passive-dependent: succorance-seeking
    d. passive-dependent: apathetic

24. Which theory deals with issues of power in relation to dependency needs?
    a. disengagement theory
    b. activity theory
    c. social reconstruction theory
    d. exchange theory

25. According to social reconstruction theory, negative changes in the self-concept are caused by
    a. society's expectations and labels.
    b. mistreatment by family members.
    c. apathy about their life due to inactivity.
    d. problems with their health.

THINKING CRITICALLY ABOUT YOUR DEVELOPMENT

Integrate material from the chapter with your own developmental experiences to respond to the following items.

1. In your own experience, what are the advantages and disadvantages of being single?

2. Describe your experiences of gender roles in dating.

3. The text lists five different types of love. Have you experienced each of these? Have you experienced all five with the same person? Discuss.

4. According to the text, six studies have concluded that marital happiness contributes more to overall personal happiness than does any other kind of satisfaction, including satisfaction from work. Do you agree? Explain.

5. The two major psychosocial tasks of early adulthood are to mold an identity and to choose and consolidate a career. Evaluate your progress on achieving these tasks.

ANSWER KEY

APPLICATIONS

1. exchange
2. disengagement
3. social reconstruction
4. cohabitation
5. postparental years
6. homogamy
7. friendship
8. burnout
9. date rape
10. family life cycle
11. activity
12. personality and lifestyle
13. consummate
14. altruistic
15. erotic

MULTIPLE CHOICE

1.	c	6.	a	11.	d	16.	b	21.	b
2.	a	7.	c	12.	c	17.	a	22.	c
3.	d	8.	b	13.	a	18.	b	23.	c
4.	c	9.	b	14.	c	19.	b	24.	d
5.	a	10.	c	15.	a	20.	a	25.	a

Chapter 20
DEATH, DYING, AND BEREAVEMENT

CHAPTER OUTLINE & OVERVIEW

I. Leading causes of death - Heart disease is the number one killer in the United States, followed by cancer. The causes of death have changed radically in the past 100 years.

II. Attitudes towards death and dying

    A. Cultural antecedents - The dominant feature of death in the twentieth century has been its invisibility. In our society, we often hide or deny death, which can sometimes prevent acceptance and positive adjustments.

    B. Criticisms - Currently, there is a swing away from the denial of death toward the notion of death with dignity.

III. Aspects of death

    A. What is death? - A distinction can be made between physiological death, clinical death, sociological death, and psychic death.

    B. Attitudes among different age groups of adults - Middle-aged respondents express the greatest fear of death; the elderly express the least.

    C. Attitudes among the elderly - The elderly are often more philosophical, more realistic, and less anxious about death than are others in our culture.

    D. Patterns of death - Pattison outlined five patterns of death:
        1. In pattern one, the terminal phase begins when the person starts to give up.
        2. In pattern two, other people reject the patient and withdraw long before death occurs.
        3. In pattern three, both the patient and others refuse to accept impending death.
        4. In pattern four, the patient rejects life and becomes psychically dead.
        5. In pattern five, there is social denial of the fact that both psychic and clinical death have occurred, and the patient is kept physiologically alive by artificial means.

IV. Varying circumstances of death

    A. Uncertain death - The circumstances of uncertain death can be very stressful for the individual and people who are close to him or her.

B. Certain death
1. Kubler-Ross identified five stages of dying that did not necessarily occur in a regular sequence: denial, anger, bargaining, depression, and acceptance.
2. According to Pattison, in between a period of crisis and the knowledge of death is the living-dying interval, which can be divided into three phases: the acute crisis phase, the chronic living-dying phase, and the terminal phase.
3. Dying people have a number of needs, and usually have a number of tasks to complete.
4. Most people agree that patients have a right to know that they are dying, but how the patients are told must be dealt with on an individual basis.

C. Untimely death: premature death
1. The psychological reactions to death are more extreme when death occurs in childhood or at a comparatively young age.
2. Sudden infant death syndrome (SIDS) is the most common cause of death in infants between 2 weeks and 1 year of age.

D. Untimely death: unexpected death - The emotional impact on survivors is gauged by how vital, alive, and distinctive the person is at the time of death.

E. Untimely death: calamitous death - Calamitous death is not only unpredictable, but it can be violent, destructive, demeaning, and even degrading. It includes accidents, involuntary manslaughter, homicide, and suicide.

F. Calamitous death: homicide - Most of the stereotypes about murder and murderers have no foundation in fact. Homicide is most often an outgrowth of quarrels and violence among family members or friends.

G. Calamitous death: suicide
1. Suicide rate increases with increasing age. Females attempt suicide more frequently than do males, but more males than females complete the suicide.
2. Older people who attempt suicide fail much less often than younger people, and any threats or symptoms must be taken seriously.

H. Socially accelerated dying - In the broadest sense, socially accelerated dying is allowing any condition or action of society that shortens life and hastens death, such as industrial pollution. In a narrow sense, it includes withholding health care from the elderly or abandoning them in nursing homes or institutions.

V. Euthanasia

    A. Meaning - Euthanasia can be described as a positive/active process (forcing a person to die) or a negative/passive process (doing nothing).

    B. Death with dignity - Death with dignity allows a terminally ill patient to die naturally without mechanized prolongation that could turn death into an ordeal.

    C. A living will - Living wills usually apply only when the person's condition is incurable. They direct in such cases that life-extending procedures be withdrawn or withheld.

    D. Mercy killing - Mercy killing is positive, direct euthanasia, either voluntary or involuntary. Mercy killing also includes abandonment or withdrawal of ordinary medical care.

    E. Death selection - Opponents of euthanasia are especially concerned about death selection, the involuntary or even mandatory killing of persons who are no longer considered socially useful, or who are judged to be a burden on society.

VI. Bereavement

    A. Grief reactions - Grief reactions are dealt with on four levels: physical, emotional, intellectual, and sociological.

    B. The stages of grief - There are usually three stages of grief: a short period of shock, a period of intense suffering, and a gradual reawakening of interest in life.

    C. Gender differences - Men have been conditioned not to show their emotions. Women not only have more friends than men, but women more often use these friends as supports in time of loss.

    D. Cultural differences - Cultural differences, such as religious beliefs, play a part in how people cope with death.

LEARNING OBJECTIVES/STUDY QUESTIONS

After reading this chapter, you should be able to:

1. Summarize the leading causes of death today.

2. Discuss the attempts to make death invisible, to deny its fact.

3. Describe the attitudes toward death among middle-aged and older adults.

4. Define the following aspects of death:

    a. physiological death -

    b. clinical death -

    c. sociological death -

    d. psychic death -

5. Summarize Pattison's five patterns of death.

   a.

   b.

   c.

   d.

   e.

6. Summarize the varying circumstances of death and the adjustments needed under each circumstance.

7. Identify the five stages of dying as outlined by Kubler-Ross.

   a.

   b.

   c.

   d.

   e.

8. Describe the living-dying trajectory as outlined by Pattison.

9. Distinguish between disintegrated and integrated dying.

10. Describe the needs of the terminally ill.

11. Discuss the emotional impact on the following types of untimely death:

    a. Premature death -

    b. Unexpected death -

    c. Calamitous death -

12. List factors contributing to adolescent suicide.

13. Examine theories of suicide.

14. Describe the different types of socially accelerated dying.

15. Define euthanasia and the following concepts: death with dignity, mercy killing, and death selection.

16. Describe the four levels of grief reactions:

    a. physical –

    b. emotional –

    c. intellectual –

    d. sociological -

17. Discuss gender differences in relation to grief.

18. Identify the three stages of grief.

19. Discuss the reactions of children to grief.

20. Describe cultural differences in relation to grief.

KEY TERMS

In your own words, provide a definition for each of the following terms:

1. Physiological death _____

_____

2. Clinical death _____

_____

3. Sociological death _____

_____

4. Psychic death _____

_____

5. Hospice _____

_____

6. Living-dying interval _____

_____

7. Disintegrated dying _____

_____

8. Integrated dying _____

_____

9. Sudden infant death syndrome _____

_____

10. Socially accelerated dying _____

_____

11. Euthanasia _____

_____

12. Death with dignity _____

_____

13. Living will _____

_____

14. Mercy killing _____

_____

15. Death selection _____

_____

16. Idealization _____

_____

APPLICATIONS

For each of the following, fill in the blank with one of the terms listed above.

1. When the patient accepts death and regresses into the self, _____ death has occurred.

2. When Maria checked on her 2-month-old baby, she found him dead in his crib. He had been a healthy baby, and she had no reason to suspect that he was ill. He may have died from _____.

3. After Mark's elderly mother was rushed to the hospital, one of the choices that Mark had to make was whether his mother should be hooked up to various life support machines. Since she had no hope of recovery and she had previously told Mark that she would not want to be kept alive under these conditions, Mark chose not to have any artificial life supports used so that his mother could have _____.

4. After a serious accident, Deb's brain ceased to exhibit any activity, although other parts of her body could continue to function if aided by life support machines. Deb could be said to have experienced _____ death but not _____ death.

5. Marjorie made up a _____ in case she was ever in a situation where someone had to decide whether to keep her alive even though there was little or no chance of recovery. In it she specified that she would not want life-sustaining procedures to be done when there was no reasonable expectation of recovery.

6. The act of allowing a person to die naturally without life support or actively putting to death a person who suffers from an incurable disease is called _____.

7. When Dan learned that he was dying, at first he became very upset. Gradually, however, he began to deal with his impending death and decided to live life to the fullest while he could. Although sometimes he didn't feel well enough to do anything and he would sometimes be depressed, at other times, he was able to continue with his life and often enjoy himself. This is an example of _____ dying.

8. Because dying in a hospital away from family members can be painful, lonely, and depressing, many people choose to go to a _____, where they are made to feel as comfortable as possible with their family members present.

9. Mark's wife was dying of cancer and was in great pain. She had no hope of recovery, and had expressed to him that she no longer wanted to live in this condition. Mark gave her some pills that killed her, believing this to be the most humane way to deal with the situation and what she wanted. This is an example of _____.

10. When Ellen was told she had just a few months to live, she went to pieces emotionally and was not able to function. This is an example of _____ dying.

11. When Valerie was 85 years old, she was put into a nursing home where family members visited her occasionally. After a few years, she became terminally ill. Her family members quickly stopped visiting her although she did not die for another few years. Before her physiological death, Valerie could be said to have experienced _____ death.

12. According to Pattison, the interval between learning about impending death and the death itself is the _____.

13. Any society that allows pollution to escalate in a way that can threaten public health, potentially shortening lives, is contributing to _____.

14. The involuntary or mandatory killing of a person who is no longer socially useful is called _____.

15. The attempt to purify the memory of the deceased is called _____.

SELF-TEST MULTIPLE CHOICE QUESTIONS

Circle the best answer for each question.

1. What is the leading cause of death in the United States?
    a. cancer
    b. homicide
    c. AIDS
    d. heart disease

2. What is the leading cause of death in children less than 4 years old in developing countries?
    a. diphteria
    b. measles
    c. scarlet fever
    d. acute infectious gastroenteritis with vomiting

3. Which of the following individuals is likely to express the greatest fear of death?
    a. 16-year-old
    b. 25-year-old
    c. 50-year-old
    d. 70-year-old

4. A child who believes that death is temporary and reversible is likely to be between the ages of
    a. 3 to 5.
    b. 5 to 9.
    c. 9 to 12.
    d. 13 to 15.

5. The cessation of all brain activity defines
    a. clinical death.
    b. psychic death.
    c. physiological death.
    d. sociological death.

6. A patient who knows that he is going to die and withdraws from the world, regressing into the self, can be said to have experienced a
    a. physiological death.
    b. clinical death.
    c. sociological death.
    d. psychic death.

7. One of the most difficult aspects of dealing with uncertain death is
    a. knowing that someone else created the painful situation.
    b. knowing that the doctors cannot help in this situation.
    c. dealing with the guilt.
    d. waiting for the outcome.

8. After Greg acknowledged that the doctors were correct about his terminal cancer, he became very hostile and bitter. He began arguing with his family and his health care providers about everything they did. Greg is in what stage of dying?
    a. denial
    b. anger
    c. depression
    d. acceptance

9. Gordie, age 45, promises that if God will just give him six months more to live, he will give up smoking and be a better husband. This reflects what stage of dying?
    a. denial
    b. anger
    c. bargaining
    d. acceptance

10. Jodi is dying from a rare blood disorder, but insists that her doctor has made a mistake in his diagnosis. According to Kubler-Ross, what stage of dying is Jodi experiencing?
    a. anger
    b. denial
    c. bargaining
    d. depression

11. Kubler-Ross was one of the first to study the topic of
    a. retirement.
    b. hospice care.
    c. euthanasia.
    d. death and dying.

12. Which of the following is *not* a phase of the living-dying interval?
    a. acute crisis phase
    b. chronic living-dying phase
    c. terminal phase
    d. acceptance phase

13. Rupert became so depressed after finding out that he was dying that he could no longer deal with daily functioning. He stopped eating and rarely got himself out of bed, even though physically he was still healthy enough to do so. He lost the will to live, and just let himself become sicker and sicker. According to Pattison, this is an example of
    a. integrated dying.
    b. disintegrated dying.
    c. disillusionment.
    d. chronic depression.

14. Which of the following is generally considered to be the best philosophy when it comes to telling patients they are dying?
    a. A patient should always be told that they are dying even if it would create enormous stress and shock which could harm them.
    b. If a person appears to be leading a happy life and there isn't anything that can be done to save them, they shouldn't be told they are dying because it could shorten the life-span.
    c. In general, every patient has the right to know that they are dying, but each case should be considered individually for when and what they should be told.
    d. It is always better to tell a family member first and let them decide when and how the patient should be told that they are dying.

15. What is the most common cause of death in infants between 2 weeks and 1 year?
    a. rubella
    b. chromosomal abnormalities
    c. meningitis
    d. sudden infant death syndrome

16. Which of the following statements about suicide is *true*?
    a. Females and males attempt suicide at the same rate, but males are more likely to actually kill themselves.
    b. Females and males attempt suicide at the same rate, but females are more likely to actually kill themselves.
    c. Females attempt suicide more often than do males, but males are more likely to complete the suicide.
    d. Males attempt suicide more often than do females, but females are more likely to complete the suicide.

17. Which of the following is an example of a condition that can lead to socially accelerated dying?
    a. industrial pollution that is not controlled
    b. unhealthy work conditions
    c. exposure to radiation
    d. All of the answers are correct.

18. Which of the following allows a terminally ill person to die naturally without putting them on machines that prolong life but may be a terrible ordeal?
    a. death with dignity
    b. mercy killing
    c. death selection
    d. active euthanasia

19. If a person would like to specify that life-sustaining procedures be withdrawn if there is no hope for recovery, they should
    a. tell a family member that this is what they prefer.
    b. tell their family physician that this is what they prefer.
    c. write up a living will.
    d. include this preference in their last will and testament.

20. What is the major difference between mercy killing and death with dignity?
    a. Mercy killing is a type of euthanasia whereas death with dignity is not.
    b. Death with dignity is undertaken to relieve a person of suffering, whereas mercy killing is not.
    c. Death with dignity allows for a natural death, while mercy killing is an active process.
    d. Death with dignity is undertaken by the hospital staff, whereas mercy killing is done by a family member or close friend.

21. Which type of euthanasia causes the most concern for the aged, and for people with severe handicaps or mental retardation?
    a. mercy killing
    b. death selection
    c. death with dignity
    d. living will

22. According to a study of grief reactions, the most common psychological grief reaction is
    a. thinking or talking about the patient.
    b. questioning the fairness of death.
    c. an increase in illnesses.
    d. feeling relieved when the ordeal is over.

23. Idealization is a(n) _____ reaction to grief.
    a. physical
    b. emotional
    c. intellectual
    d. sociological

24. What is a common intellectual reaction to bereavement?
    a. denial
    b. bargaining
    c. death selection
    d. idealization

25. What occurs during the first stage of grief?
   a. The bereaved feel as if they are in a state of shock.
   b. The bereaved show physical and emotional symptoms of great disturbance.
   c. There is a painful longing for the dead.
   d. There is a gradual reawakening of interest in life.

THINKING CRITICALLY ABOUT YOUR DEVELOPMENT

Integrate material from the chapter with your own developmental experiences to respond to the following items.

1. What attempts have you witnessed to make death invisible?

2. What is your attitude about death? How have your conceptions of death changed with age?

3. Is the research on gender differences in grief true for you? Explain.

4. What are your views on euthanasia? Discuss death with dignity, mercy killing, and death selection.

5. Have you experienced grief over the loss of a loved one? What stages of grief did you experience? What different levels of grief reaction did you experience?

ANSWER KEY

APPLICATIONS

1. psychic
2. sudden infant death syndrome
3. death with dignity
4. clinical, physiological
5. living will
6. euthanasia
7. integrated
8. hospice
9. mercy killing
10. disintegrated
11. sociological
12. living-dying interval
13. socially accelerated dying
14. death selection
15. idealization

MULTIPLE CHOICE

1. c
2. d
3. c
4. a
5. a
6. d
7. d
8. b
9. c
10. b
11. d
12. d
13. b
14. c
15. c
16. c
17. d
18. a
19. c
20. c
21. b
22. a
23. c
24. d
25. a